Victorian Values

Victorian Values

The Life and Times of

Dr. Edwin Lankester

M.D., F.R.S.

Mary P English

Biopress Ltd

ISBN 0-948737-14-X

PUBLISHED BY:

Biopress Ltd.
"The Orchard"
Clanage Road
Bristol BS3 2JX
England

British Library Cataloguing in Publication Data

English, Mary P.
    Victorian values: the life and times of Dr Edwin
    Lankester, M.D., F.R.S.
    1. Great Britain. Science, history. Lankester, Edwin 1814-
    1874
    I. Title
    509.42092

    ISBN 0-948737-14-X

Printed in Hong Kong by Dah Hua Printing Press Co. Ltd.

Contents

List of Illustrations

Acknowledgements

So many librarians, archivists and historians contributed their expert knowledge to this book that it is impossible to name them all. A few are mentioned in the text, and to them, to those listed below, and to many others, my grateful thanks are due.

Dr. D. E. Allen (Wellcome Trust) gave me continual encouragement and put me in touch with Edwin Lankester's descendants, Dr. Peter Lankester and Dr. Hugh Lankester. Concerning the Lankester family and Edwin's childhood I learned much from Woodbridge Library (Mr. J. Harrington), Mr. M. Weaver of Seckford Grammar School, Woodbridge, and the Suffolk Record Office, Ipswich: my cousins, Miss R. English and Mrs. M. Howes were most helpful.

Saffron Walden Library, the Library of University College, London, Doncaster Central Library and the Ruprecht-Karl University, Heidelberg (Dr. Weisert) provided much information on Lankester's career before he settled in London.

For details of his career as scientist, teacher, medical officer of health and coroner, and for background information, I am indebted to the skill and patience of the staff of the following libraries, archives and museums: the University Library, the Medical Library and the Biology Library of Bristol University; the Bristol Central Library; the Greater London Record Office; the Archives and Local Studies Department of the Victoria Library, Westminster (Miss M. J. Swarbrick); the Library of the Royal College of Physicians (Mr. G. Davenport); the Local Studies Departments of the Central Library, Islington and of Marylebone Library; the Wellcome Library; the Science Museum Library; the Victoria and Albert Museum; the Linnean Society Library (Miss G. Douglas); Dr. Williams's Library (Mr. J. Creasy); the Royal Archives, Windsor Castle (Lady de Bellaigue); Dickens House Museum; the National Museums of Scotland (for the William Jardine papers).

The following individuals gave me the benefit of their expert knowledge in their specialist fields: Mr. P. S. Green of the Royal Botanic Gardens, Kew; Mr. J. D. K. Burton of the Coroners' Society; Mr. R. Caldwell; Dr. L. Greenham of the University of Bristol; Dr. E. Williams of

xi

Bristol Royal Infirmary; Mr. J. Morrell of the University of Bradford; Dr. I. Loudon, Dr. D. Porter and Dr. A. Hardy, medical historians.

I am grateful to the Wellcome Trust for a grant in aid of research expenses and illustrations.

Mrs G. E. Lockett kindly compiled the index.

Note: Since completing the manuscript of this book, I have learnt that some of Edwin Lankester's diaries, written during the childhood of his son, Ray, are still in existence in private hands. Unfortunately I have not been allowed to see them.

Foreword

Edwin Lankester was above all an outsider, a non-conformist for whom life was one long unremitting battle against what it is now fashionable to call "the Establishment" - medical, social, commercial and juridical. His mother was an impoverished widow, he left school at the age of 12. He had to struggle to find the resources to qualify as an apothecary and a surgeon. He was forced by circumstances to graduate abroad, although he could hardly have done better than to choose Heidelberg. Subsequently, he was thwarted in his ambition to become a consultant physician in London by reason of the extraordinary qualifications required by the Royal College of Physicians at that time.

Nevertheless, Lankester took such opportunities as arose, first to become apprenticed to a local apothecary and later to become tutor to the children of a benevolent landowner. He learned his German from a fellow tutor, and used the countryside around him to become a botanist of such repute as to be elected Fellow of the Royal Society at the early age of 31. He proceeded to become a pioneering Medical Officer of Health and a fearless coroner. He accepted every invitation to teach, write and edit, and to become an outstanding communicator at every level. Undoubtedly, if fate had decreed that he follow a conventional career in either science or medicine, he could not have hoped to achieve so much.

It was doubtless logical in psychological terms that Lankester should have been driven to become an active member of every scientific and medical society dedicated to reform and to education of the public. He was blessed with a magnetic personality and with awesome physical and spiritual energy, and his influence on those around him was clearly incalculable.

It was essentially as a scientist that Lankester served the medical profession - still scientifically in its infancy - and the public weal. He was untiring in his advocacy and practical demonstrations of the value of scientific methods, whether in seeking to measure contamination of a water supply, or ozone in the atmosphere, in applying basic statistics to an understanding of the causes of mortality and morbidity, or in pursuing the beguiling theory of a fungoid cause of cholera. His labours for the scientific community were prodigious, notably through his honorary secretaryship of the botany and zoology section of the British Association for the Advancement of Science throughout a momentous quarter century, and his success, as editor, in establishing the *Quarterly Journal of Microscopical Science*, in which his son, Edwin Ray, was to join and later succeed him.

The main value of Mary English's sparkling and scholarly study is, however, that of any truly vital biography; that is the light it sheds upon the contemporary scene. No time in remembered history is of greater moment for the scientist - natural, physical or social - or the doctor - especially in public health - or, indeed, any humanitarian individual, than the era of Edwin Lankester. How fitting is the title - "Victorian Values" - at a time when dewy-eyed political sentimentalists depict as a nostalgic Elysium an age which was in reality a living hell for most of Her Majesty's liege subjects. New light is cast upon aspects of the Reform and Sanitary Era, to the delight of the amateur and, I suspect, even the professional historian. There is the graphic depiction of internecine strife within the emerging medical profession, whose Augean Stables Lankester did so much to cleanse. There is the salutary and sadly familiar saga of the uses of new technology, notably the stethoscope and the microscope: particularly how the latter led early histologists into error because the wish was father to the thought that "particles" causing cholera could be seen decades before staining techniques allowed Koch to demonstrate the vibrio. There is the belated recognition of Lankester's crucial contribution to facilitating Snow's classic detective work. There is the stark evidence of the importance of enlightened self-interest in the calculating way in which, as a shrewd Medical Officer of Health, Lankester appealed to the mercenary instincts of his employers in one of the wealthiest - probably unhealthiest - parishes in London. There is the distressing account of the parsimony and vindictiveness of the Justices of the Peace whose one objective appeared to be the intimidation of the coroner, whom they had the power to ruin.

The enigma of Lankester's obscurity may be explained largely by his being eclipsed by the brilliance of his son, Sir Edwin Ray Lankester, who benefited from a happy and stimulating upbringing. Yet it probably owed more to the brutal selectivity of historical judgement, which highlights the single striking achievement to the depreciation of the many seminal acts of personal and public service of an Edwin Lankester.

Alexander W. Macara
Consultant Senior Lecturer
in Public Health Medicine.
Chairman, Representative Body of
the British Medical Association (1990)

Introduction

Edwin Lankester's career as a medical man and biologist spans a period in which revolutionary change was taking place, not only in basic scientific knowledge, but in the organisation of the professions of both medicine and science. His medical career began when, as a poverty-stricken 12 year-old, he was apprenticed to a country surgeon, but he went on, through his own efforts, to qualify at the newly opened University of London and at Heidelberg University. However, he was refused membership of the Royal College of Physicians, ultimately because he was not of a sufficiently elevated social standing. Despite this, he counted the Queen's physician, Sir James Clark, among his friends, and edited a book for Prince Albert. He died a bankrupt, having exhausted his slender means in the fight for the (then elected) coronership of Central Middlesex. His life was devoted to a struggle against the private affluence, the public squalor, the greed and self-seeking, which were the hallmarks of the times. First as elected vestryman (i.e. parish counsellor), and later as the first Medical Officer of Health, both in the parish of St. James's, Westminster, he fought for the alleviation of the appalling conditions endured by the slum dwellers of the north of the parish: as Coroner, he managed to extend the fight to the whole of Central Middlesex, using publicity as his most potent weapon.

Lankester was a competent biologist as well as a doctor, and for many years he was an active member of the British Association for the Advancement of Science and of the Microscopical Society of London. He was a brilliant lecturer and an accomplished and very popular writer of science for the layman, who believed that only if the public, and especially women, could be taught the principles of nutrition, child care, and the prevention of spread of epidemic disease, could the dreadful mortality of the times be conquered.

Edwin Lankester is forgotten today, though he is sometimes mistaken for his better known son, Sir Ray Lankester. Yet in his time his name was seldom out of the medical press, he had a large circle of friends from Charles Dickens to Thomas Henry Huxley, and his activities as Medical Officer of Health and Coroner were widely reported and discussed, in London at least. He is one of the forgotten giants of the Victorian reform movement whose life story offers a revealing picture of the true nature of the much vaunted "Victorian values", values which ultimately led to the premature death of one who was rash enough to fight them.

Chapter One

Suffolk Childhood   1814-1832

The pleasant market town of Woodbridge lies on the west bank of the River Deben, about 13 miles up from its mouth on the flat Suffolk coast. The river is still tidal at Woodbridge, and its waters brackish. The town boasts a tide-mill which now, as in the last century, is a local landmark and, along with numerous windmills, one or two of which still stand, must have been kept very busy grinding corn for the townspeople. At that time Woodbridge was a centre for farming, its river port traded coal and corn, there were boat-builders' yards, and its position on the direct coaching route from Yarmouth to London ensured that it was a thriving community.

The town's main street, the Thoroughfare, lies parallel to the river; from it, Quay Street runs eastward down to the river, and Church Street westwards past the fine, flint-faced, fifteenth century St. Mary's Church and up to Market Hill with its Shire Hall, given to the town in the sixteenth century by its great benefactor, Thomas Seckford (Fig. 1). At the north end of the Thoroughfare the shops peter out and a mile or two further on the road becomes the single street of the small village of Melton (Fig. 2). Here was born, to William and Susan Lankester, on 23 April, 1814, a son, Edwin.

Both William and Susan came from Woodbridge. At that time Lankester was a common enough name in the district, members of the family including farmers, a butcher and a chandler; but William, according to his entry in the Register of Burials, was a builder*. The occupation of Susan's father, Robert Taylor, is unknown, though an Alfred Taylor, who may have been a relative, was a well-known local hairdresser and town gossip[1]. William and Susan were married by Special Licence at St. Mary's Church on New Year's Day, 1814, the need for the Special Licence being explained by the fact that Edwin was born only three months later,[2] after

---

* When Edwin married he entered his father's occupation on his marriage certificate as "Architect". Whether this was a harmless attempt to enhance his own social status, or whether he had been brought up to believe it, we can only guess.

Fig. 1. Market Hill and the Shire Hall, Woodbridge.

Fig. 2. The Melton road, Woodbridge.

the couple had moved to Melton. An infant daughter, younger that Edwin, is mentioned by some sources, but I have been able to find no further mention of her. However, another child was conceived about three years after the wedding, but early in January, 1818, before it was born, William died of tuberculosis aged only 27. He was buried in the graveyard of Quay Street Congregational Chapel, Woodbridge (Fig. 3), on 11 January,[3] and a month later his infant son was born, died, and was buried in the same graveyard; the widowed Susan was left to bring up four-year-old Edwin alone. William left a small property which should have helped to support them, but its injudicious use left Susan penniless, and Edwin was brought up in very straitened circumstances. It seems strange that no relatives were apparently prepared to help the little family, though it is possible that Edwin's conception out of wedlock still rankled with them.

Fig. 3. Quay Street Congregational Chapel, Woodbridge, in 1989.

The child's schooling is a matter of some conjecture. All sources agree that what education he received was in Woodbridge, and most imply if they do not actually state, that he attended Woodbridge School, that is, Seckford Grammar School, Woodbridge, the fine red brick Victorian building which stands in its own grounds just outside and above the town. Now, though it stems from a very old foundation, neither the Grammar School nor its buildings existed in Edwin's childhood. Its immediate fore-runner was the Free School, part of the Charity raised for the town by

Fig. 4. The Royal Oak Inn, in the Thoroughfare, Woodbridge.

Thomas Seckford, the donor of the Shire Hall. The Free School was housed in a modest building of the 1660s in Seckford Street, at the top of Market Hill and, as its name implies, took in a number of free scholars from the town as well as paying pupils.[4] It was not until the 1860s that the Seckford Charity agreed with some town worthies that the necessary expansion of the Free School could not possibly take place on its then site, and it was replaced by the Grammar School in its present buildings, which opened in 1865. If Edwin attended the Free School, he must have been one of the Free Scholars but, though there are some Lankesters on the school roll, or *Liber Admissionem*, all were before Edwin's time. Even if he did attend the school (which would have been from approximately 1822 to 1826) it seems he would have gained little from his stay, for between 1815 and 1832 the school, which had been very highly thought of, was at its lowest ebb. Its buildings were in such a state of disrepair that rooms had to be hired in the town, and successive head masters neglected the free pupils to lavish their attention on the fee-paying boys.[4] However, there were two other schools in the town at the time, a National (Church of England) School, taking 150 pupils, and a Congregational School, presumably attached to the Quay Street Chapel.[5] As William Lankester had been buried in the Chapel graveyard, it must be presumed that he belonged to the sect, so that it would be more natural that his son should be educated by that sect than by a Church of England foundation*. I believe that historians and obituarists knowing, when he died, that there was a grammar school in Woodbridge, have jumped to the conclusion that Edwin must have attended it, but that it is much more likely that he was educated at the Congregational School.

When Edwin reached the age of twelve his mother could no longer afford to keep him at school and it was decided to apprentice him to a watchmaker but fortunately, in view of his subsequent career, before this could be arranged Samuel Gissing, a surgeon of Market Hill, agreed to take him on as an apprentice. His mother then moved back to Woodbridge where she kept the Royal Oak, an inn (long closed) in the Thoroughfare, at its junction with Oak Lane (Fig. 4).

---

* The fact that he was married in St. Mary's Church does not contradict this assumption, as marriages were only recognised at the time if registered with the Church of England.

Chapter Two

Physician in Training   1832-1837

Edwin Lankester's medical career spanned an era of radical change in the organisation and regulation of the profession and in the training of doctors, which culminated in the Medical Reform Act of 1858 on which modern procedure is based. He himself was to play an important part in the formulation of that Act.

At the beginning of the nineteenth century qualified medical men were still, as they had been for 200 years, split into three sharply demarcated estates - physicians, surgeons and apothecaries - separated as strictly by social class as by their medical function. Only the physicians were graduates and therefore gentlemen, accepted as equals by churchmen, lawyers and other professional men. They were organized by their own Royal College of Physicians which had received its Royal Charter from Henry VIII. Though graduates of Scottish and Irish Universities could be licenced to practice by the College, only Oxford and Cambridge men were admitted as Fellows; and as these Universities had a religious test, Fellowship, and therefore government of the College, was restricted to members of the Church of England. There were comparatively few physicians, and their social standing meant that their practice was largely confined to the well off, for the poor could in no way afford their fees. Clearly the youthful Edwin, son of a poverty stricken widow, could have little hope of becoming a physician.

Surgeons, who until 1745 had been organized with the barbers in the Barber-Surgeons' Company of the City of London, and did not split away to form their own Royal College of Surgeons until 1800, were still considered to be craftsmen whose trade was essentially that of a skilled manual labourer. Consequently, they had no need of a University education; like other craftsmen they received a purely practical training as apprentices or pupils, qualifying as Members of the College (MRCS), and thus their social standing was considerably inferior to that of the physicians. Many poor boys were apprenticed to surgeons not because they had any special bent for the medical profession, but because the training was comparatively cheap, most apprenticeships involving minimal or no fees. As well as performing operations, surgeons set fractures, treated accident cases, and attended to skin disorders and some gynaecological problems. It is not known what Edwin's ambitions were when he took up his apprenticeship to Mr. Gissing at the tender age of twelve, but if he was genuinely interested he may already have heard that a few poor apprentices had somehow managed to teach themselves enough Latin, Greek, Chemistry and Botany to gain entrance to a University later on.

The third medical estate comprised the apothecaries, organized in the Society of Apothecaries which had received its Royal Charter in 1617. These men were primarily druggists who made up and sold over the counter the medicines prescribed by the physicians. They were thus classified socially as tradesmen and, like the surgeons, were inferior to the physicians. Like the surgeons too, their training was through apprenticeship to a qualified practitioner. At first apothecaries were entitled only to dispense drugs, but the inaccessibility of the physicians to the great mass of the population led gradually to the apothecaries taking on diagnostic and prescribing responsibilities for the less well-off until, in 1815, the Apothecaries' Act legitimised the practice and entitled the Society to grant to its members a licence, the Licence of the Society of Apothecaries (L.S.A.), to practise in England. Meanwhile, many surgeons were finding it impossible to earn a living by surgery alone and were qualifying as apothecaries as well, so achieving a status approximating to that of a general practitioner, though it was a little while before a profession so named came into existence. However, their social status remained low, and as late as 1858 a general practitioner writing in the *Lancet* could complain: "Medicine is not looked on as the profession of a gentleman ... our wives are not visitable ... the great body of the profession is looked on by the upper classes as about a shade better than respectable tradespeople."[1]

Compulsory registration of doctors only began with the Act of 1858, and until that time, in addition to practitioners with recognized qualifications, large numbers of herbalists, chiropractors, healers, pedlers and quacks of all sorts roamed the country, sold their wares and gave medical advice without let or hindrance to anyone prepared to listen. Indeed, in the countryside the advice of a local woman well versed in the properties of herbs was greatly respected. A little later in the century homoeopaths were much in evidence, and Lankester would denounce them virulently on a number of occasions.

Such was the state of the medical profession at the beginning of the century, but by the time that the young Edwin was articled in 1826, change had already begun, and the basis of that change was the rise of scientific medicine, the foundation of which was the remarkable achievement of the great British surgeon, John Hunter (1728-1793), and his studies of comparative anatomy and physiology. Now, for the first time, treatment could be based on the signs observed by the doctor, and not exclusively on the symptoms described by the patient as had, up to then, been the rule. Until that time a physician rarely examined his patient, for there was little he could learn by so doing; but when observations could be more precise, for instance, with the introduction of the stethoscope in 1819, medicine began to be a science rather than an art. Coincidentally, the status of surgeons relative to physicians began to rise, for the former could no longer be classed as mere craftsmen now that book learning, even though excluding the classical learning of the physician, was becoming an essential part of their training. Despite this, training by apprenticeship or pupillage only died out slowly, and was still in existence when the 1858 Act came on to the statute book: it has, in fact, never been formally abolished.

Living in a small market town as he did, Edwin's first master, Samuel Gissing, though described as a surgeon, is unlikely to have confined his practice to surgery. It is more probable that he held the double qualification of MRCS, LSA, running a general practice and dispensing and selling the drugs he prescribed. Thus in the six years which Edwin spent with him on Market Hill the boy would have had a wide experience of his future trade, even if some of his time was spent on menial tasks such as cleaning the premises and running errands.

When his articles expired in 1832 Edwin left Suffolk, never to return to live there, moving to Fareham, Hampshire, where he became assistant to a surgeon named Stanisland. But he was very badly treated there and left after a few months to become an assistant at the Repertorium, Seymour Street, Euston Square, in London*. Here bad luck dogged him still, he suffered literally from semi-starvation, and moved on rapidly becoming, in his nineteenth year, assistant to Mr. Thomas Spurgin, General Practitioner of Saffron Walden, Essex. By all accounts Mr. Spurgin was a remarkable man, and there is no doubt that it was because of the opportunities which he opened up to Edwin, and of which the latter was quick to take every advantage, that the young assistant was able to lay the foundations for his future distinguished career.

Spurgin (so spelled in contemporary documents[2]) was himself only 35 at the time, had as yet no children, and is said to have been severe, ascetic and deeply religious. But he was active in the town's affairs, and by 1851 had become a justice of the peace. He must also have been a man of means, possibly with a private income as well as that from his practice for, again by 1851, he employed a governess, three indoor servants and a groom to attend to the needs of himself, his wife, and eight children[3] (Fig. 5). Despite his reputation for asceticism, Spurgin took pleasure in furthering the intellectual development of his assistants, encouraging them to make extensive use of his own large library. Of this Edwin promptly

* I have been unable to trace any record of this establishment.

Fig. 5. Dr. Spurgin's home, The Grange, Saffron Walden. The balcony has now been taken down.

took advantage, working hard with Spurgin's help to learn Latin and Greek and study the English classics, subjects of which his brief schooling had deprived him but which would be essential if he were to attain the more exalted ranks of the medical profession.

There existed in Saffron Walden at the time a small literary society, the Mental Improvement Society, of which Spurgin was a member. About two years earlier this Society had appointed a sub-committee, including Spurgin, charged with setting up a natural history branch, mainly for the purpose of collecting specimens. Finding considerable apathy among members of the Society as a whole, the sub-committee took matters into its own hands and, in 1832, started the Saffron Walden Natural History Society, and such was the enthusiasm of its members that by the end of the year it had been resolved to set up a museum to house local natural history and antiquarian exhibits.[4] When Lankester arrived in the town in

1833 the excitement over the future museum must have been at its height and he was quickly recruited, presumably by Spurgin, into the jobs of Secretary to the Society and Curator of the Museum, though the latter had, as yet, no premises. This is the first intimation we have of Lankester's deep interest in natural history, to which much of his early career would be devoted.

Every waking moment of his brief time at Saffron Walden must have been filled (pressaging the way in which he would conduct his affairs for the rest of his life), carrying out his duties as a doctor, studying the classics, and helping to run the Society and its putative museum. He made so many friends through these activities, and his character, abilities and enthusiasm impressed those friends so much, that they clubbed together to lend him £300 to see him through the next stage in the advancement of his medical career.

Up to the 1820s Oxford and Cambridge had been the only Universities in England and, as we have seen, they would have been far beyond the reach of such as Lankester, whose Congregationalist faith would, in any case, have precluded his entry. However, in 1826 the University of London was founded as a joint stock company with a prospectus, shareholders and a Council, with the objects, first of providing a place of higher education for those unable, for whatever reason, to enter the older universities and, secondly, of offering subjects omitted from their largely classical curricula. It could not at first grant degrees. Professors were paid from students' fees rather than only by those students who chose to attend their lectures; and to reduce expense, the University was non-residential. Building had started immediately, and in October, 1828, the University (now University College, London) opened in Gower Street with 600 students attending Deprtments of Medicine, Law, Science, Engineering and Arts. Middlesex Hospital served as the teaching hospital for medical students until University College Hospital opened in 1840.[5] The University was, therefore, but six years old when Lankester, thanks to his friends at Saffron Walden, started his three-year course there in 1834, having brought his classical education up to the required standard and found lodgings close by at 32, University Street.[6]

The new University was not only non-denominational, it was non-religious; that is, religion was not taught there and played no part in its affairs. This was highly unacceptable to a number of sincerely but not dogmatically, religious educationalists who in 1828 founded, in direct opposition to "the godless establishment in Gower Street", King's College in the Strand, with a Department of Divinity but no religious test for staff or students. In 1836, while Lankester was still at the University of London, that establishment was renamed University College, London, and a new University incorporating both it and King's College was given its Charter and allowed to award degrees. So for the first time in this country, Dissenters would be able to graduate in medicine. For some time, however, the new University continued to prepare students for the MRCS and LSA examinations, for by no means all were in a position to sit for a degree.[5]

Before the founding of the University, medical students in London had been severely handicapped by the fact that there was no one place where they could obtain both their theoretical and practical training; to cover all parts of their course they had to make their own private arrangements with a number of different establishments, travelling between them and fitting them into a time-table as best they could. Hospital medical schools did not begin to appear before the 1830s; before that their place was taken by any number of totally unregulated private schools many of which sprang up and rapidly disappeared again, and only a few of which were of a high standard with recognised teachers. In particular, many of the schools did not offer instruction in anatomy because of the difficulty of obtaining bodies. The schools had no access to beds, so to obtain his clinical experience a student had to find a hospital practitioner who was willing to accept him as a pupil for a privately arranged fee, and he would then accompany his principal on the wards. Of course the best known and most skilled doctors would only accept the wealthiest and most brilliant students so that the quality of clinical teaching received by individual students varied greatly. The opening of London University changed all this, enabling many students to learn from a few gifted teachers in a set course which included theoretical, clinical and practical work, all carried out in an atmostphere of learning. Lankester was entering upon his higher education at most propitious moment, and he set about making the most of his opportunities.

As the University was not yet offering degrees, Lankester would be working for the double qualification, MRCS, LSA. In theory, such a qualification required five years of study including apprenticeship, a spell at a school or college with an examination, and hospital practice, the length of time spent on each being variable. The subjects required for the college course included anatomy, physiology, chemistry, materia medica, botany and vegetable physiology, therapeutics, principles and practice of medicine, clinical medicine, morbid anatomy, forensic medicine, midwifery and diseases of children. In practice it was not unusual for the college course and hospital practice to be run concurrently for a year, while four years were given to the apprenticeship. Study of the academic curriculum quoted above must have been sketchy indeed if it were compressed into one year while the student was also walking the wards. At London University the course was so framed that a student could obtain his double qualification in 15 months, but a four-year course was recommended. In practice, students could choose which courses they wished to attend and were not compelled to take the seasonal examinations. By deciding to spend three years at the University, Lankester, who already had five years experience as an apprentice as well as two as an assistant, would be exceptionally well qualified.

Medical students at the University had a strong and lively corporate life, encouraged by their professors who invited them every month to a *conversazione* in the Museum. The students' Medical Society, of which Lankester was President for a spell, had a membership of 150 and an income from subscriptions of £40 a year, out of which they bought books for their own library to supplement those in the University library. They paid their own librarian, and in 1836 were asking the University authorities for more space to house their books.[6] One of the Society's more important activities was the organization of paper-reading meetings for its members, so giving them invaluable experience in public speaking. It must have been here that Lankester, who had already taken his first steps on a public platform at Saffron Walden, laid the foundations for his future reputation as a skilled and popular lecturer.

It was while he was still a student, too, that his prolific writing career began. In 1836 he published in the *London Medical and Surgical Journal* a lengthy paper under the title "Essay on the Uncertainty of Medical Science, and the Numerical Method of M. Louis",[7] being the text of one he had read at a meeting of the University Medical Society in November of that year. In it he was highly critical of the subjectivity and lack of precision in the diagnosis, treatment and prognosis of disease which prevailed in the medical profession of the time, describing the state of the profession in the words of an unnamed source as follows:

> Nature is fighting with disease; a blind man armed with a club, that is the physician, comes to settle the difference. He first tries to make peace; when he cannot accomplish this, he lifts his club and strikes at random; if he strikes the disease, he kills the disease; if he strikes nature, he kills nature.

Among the causes of this situation Lankester quoted the attempt to account for the phenomena of disease by propounding fixed laws without testing these laws against facts, with the result that each physician had his own favourite set of laws. Francis Bacon's insistence on the need to found laws on fact had been adopted in all the sciences except medicine, he complained, though the large number of facts which must be taken into account in that discipline admittedly presented a problem. "The perfection of science depends on the accuracy with which we can trace the relation of cause and effect", wrote Lankester, giving the introduction of the stethoscope (only nineteen years previously) as a "splendid instance of what may be done for medicine by patient observation", given the tools. He emphasized, too, the necessity of always studying the body as a whole because of the way in which all the tissues and organs interact with one another. For instance, "How little we know of [fever's] true cause; the real state of the system in which it originates; and what symptoms and lesions are primary, and what secondary." He commented on the effect of age, sex, external circumstances and education on bodily phenomena, and "the potent influence of mind over all, increasing, suspending or modifying the varied actions of the living solid".

Next he considered the imperfect state of physiological and pathological knowledge which still could not supply the answers to such questions as: "How does mercury act in subduing inflammation? Why is lemon juice specific in scurvy? Why are tubercle and carcinoma incurable, whilst glandular swellings are easily dispersed? What are the morbid lesions in epilepsy, tetanus, chorea or hydrophobia? What are the causes of idiosyncrasies? ..." But pathology and physiology were observational disciplines: other sciences were able to test their laws experimentally but this was impossible with medicine, for animal experiments could only be an approximation. Medicine was therefore at a disadvantage compared with other sciences. Another of medicine's shortcomings was the unreliability of medical testimony, each observer giving his own, subjective, narrative description of the case before him, coloured by his own prejudices and with no standard, scientific point of reference. Lankester deplored, too, the taking as fact of what were mere statements of opinion; for instance, a patient with "scarletina" who had taken a minute dose of belladonna and recovered from his fever was sometimes stated to have been cured by the drug.

Finally he arrived at a description of the new "numerical method" of Monsieur Louis of Paris which was the focus of his paper. M. Louis had devoted seven years to collecting detailed information on 1960 patients with phthisis (pulmonary tuberculosis) and several hundred patients with other diseases, at La Charité Hospital. 450 phthisis patients died in hospital, and of these he regarded his data as sufficiently complete for his purpose in only 123 cases. First he collected every available fact, positive and negative, about the patient over the whole course of his illness and arranged them according to their progress, duration, and order and circumstances of development; then he tabulated them under symptom, order, and function affected. This allowed him to calculate the frequency of occurrence of each phenomenon in the disease, to discard those which only appeared occasionally as being of no diagnostic significance, and to obtain an accurate picture of the disease in its various phases based on universal, or near universal, symptoms only. Once an accurate picture of each disease had been thus obtained there would be no need to use this laborious method in every new case, for each could be matched to the already prepared tables. Lankester then proceeded to dispute the argument that it is impossible to reduce medicine to the rank of a true science, as the numerical method attempted to do, believing that the phenomena involved were simply more difficult to investigate than in other sciences, but were not beyond the mind of man provided that the correct methods were used.

The long preamble to this first scientific paper of his is an important statement of Lankester's philosophy and indicates that he had thought deeply about the shortcomings of his chosen profession and was looking for ways to overcome them, even before he had started on an independent medical career. It shows how early he developed the strongly scientific outlook which would be a conspicuous feature of his whole working life, though his frequent attempts at practical science, always on a small scale and not always entirely successful, suggest that he probably lacked the intellectual brilliance to become a top-ranking professional scientist. One very striking feature of this paper, especially considering its early date, is the complete absence of any reference to The Almighty; in fact, Lankester went out of his way to emphasize that problems of human illness were merely rather complex scientific problems, as soluble, with increasing knowledge, as any other scientific problem. He was still refusing to ascribe to divine intervention observations which were so far unexplained when he remarked to the British Association in 1851, *a propos* of the movement of sap in plants, that: "it is unsophisticated to speak of vitality as a force when it could not be demonstrated to exist, especially when physical forces are capable of explaining the phenomenon." In other contexts, however, his writings leave no doubt that he was a believer. He would state categorically the part played by divine intervention in creation and evolution (p. 51), and in his books for the lay public his references to The Lord, his power and his mercy, were sometimes profuse, as they were in many popular scientific writings of the day. As to M. Louis' numerical method, it was, of course, never adopted, being far too cumbersome in the days before computers, or even punched cards, existed. But present day methods of computer diagnosis are based on precisely the same premises - M. Louis and Edwin Lankester were prophets before their time.

There is one further omission from this paper which is noteworthy in view of Lankester's later preoccupation with epidemic disease and its causes. Smallpox was always epidemic at the time, and the first great cholera outbreak had swept Britain in 1831-1832, yet nowhere among the very many unresolved problems which he used to illustrate the points he raised are infectious diseases mentioned; they were not matters of interest to him at this stage of his career. His primary interest was clearly in clinical medicine and, as later developments show, it was only through a fortuitous series of events that he was finally forced to give up this idea and enter the public service.

Among the eminent professors under whom Lankester studied was the botanist, John Lindley (1799-1865) (Fig. 6), who held the post of Professor of Botany at University College from 1829 to 1860. He was a man of extraordinary energy whose watchwords were method, zeal and perseverance. His first written work, a translation from the French of a book on the structure of fruits, was completed at a single sitting of three days and two nights. Many of his more important writings, and his output was huge, were undertaken on behalf of his students. For 40 years he held posts of increasing responsibility in the Royal Horticultural Society, first in its gardens and later as an administrator, and he was also frequently consulted by the government. He was an advocate of the "natural" rather than the Linnean classification of plants, and his original researches on their structure resulted in his continually changing his mind as to their inter-relationships.

Fig. 6. Professor John Lindley.

When the College opened, botany had only been included as a subject because of the needs of the Medical School, and it was held in very low esteem. This Lindley was not prepared to tolerate and he quickly built up a respected department, even overcoming the lack of a botanic garden by using his position with the Royal Horticultural Society to obtain the use of its garden at Turnham Green for his students.[5,8] Botany was not a laboratory subject until the 1880s, so Lindley's main responsibility was to deliver 50 lectures a year to medical students, together with a few demonstrations of microscopical botany. He was an excellent lecturer, and very popular, both for the clarity and conciseness of his profusely illustrated talks and, despite his reputation for brusqueness and a hot temper, for his kindness to his students. It is recorded[8] that Lankester was "among the more distinguished" of these, and Lindley certainly thought highly of his pupil, for some years later he was to name a newly discovered plant genus after him.

Fig. 7. Distribution of prizes at University College, London, in 1843.

Lankester, who was known among his fellow students for his devotion to his studies, did well in his examinations, gaining Certificates of Honour in most subjects in his first two years. For instance, in 1835-6 he came second in pathological anatomy and botany, third in natural philosophy (i.e. physics), fourth in practice of medicine, midwifery and diseases of women and children, and seventh in surgery and medical jurisprudence; his lowest Certificate was for anatomy in which he came thireenth. Professor Lindley offered prizes in his subject in the sessional examinations (Fig. 7), and that year Lankester's performance won him the Lindley Silver Medal in Botany. In contrast, his fellow student, William Hardwicke, who would become a close associate and whose career would run parallel to Lankester's, won only two Certificates that year.[9]

In 1837 Lankester sat for the examinations for the Licence of the Society of Apothecaries and the Membership of the Royal College of Surgeons. Up to that date the Membership examination had been entirely oral and had been conducted by all nine members of the College Court sitting together. 1837 was the first year of a new, streamlined procedure in which only three members examined each candidate, but those who failed were entitled to prove themselves in a written paper, though Lankester, with all his Certificates of Honour would have had no need of this lifeline. The oral examination took place at six o'clock in the evening and included anatomy and physiology as well as medicine and surgery.[10] Lankester passed both examinations.

Chapter Three

Building a Career   1838-1845

It was not uncommon at that date for a newly qualified and impecunious young doctor to spend a year or two in the service of a "good" family, earning some money and building up lucrative contacts for a future practice. Lankester's humble origins would have precluded him from finding such a post for himself, for he would have had no family connections through which to obtain introductions. Despite this, such was the next step in his career, for through his friendship with Professor Lindley he obtained the post of tutor and medical attendant to the family of Mr Charles Wood of Campsall, a village about seven miles from Doncaster.

Lindley's choice on his protégé's behalf was inspired, for the Woods, an eccentric family who had rented Campsall Hall a few years before, had interests which exactly complemented Lankester's. The household consisted of Mr. Wood himself, his wife, three sons, Neville, Willoughby and Charles junior, and three daughters. The sons were young men at the time of Lankester's arrival; Neville had already published three books on natural history. Lankester was employed, in his own words, to conduct "the studies of the three young gentlemen through a complete course of medical education giving them practical instruction in connection with a public dispensary".[1] Nothing is known of Mrs. Wood or her daughters except that they were recluses who seldom strayed beyond the grounds of the Hall. Nevertheless, like their menfolk, they had a passion for education which they indulged in an extremely expensive manner. Housing them in the village, the Woods employed professors of French, German and Spanish, and a music master, to bring culture and knowledge to the family. Lankester, as tutor to the sons, joined this group. All augmented their incomes by giving lessons to the local inhabitants, and the foreigners among them scandalized "the neighbouring clergy who saw havoc being made among the flowers of their congregations".[2]

Lankester lost no time in throwing himself into the intellectual life of the district. The men of the Wood family were active members of the Doncaster Lyceum, a literary and scientific society in the neighbouring town, with wide interests, and their tutor soon joined them. By May, 1838, he was taking part in the discussion of a literary talk given by Willoughby Wood, a young man with a musical bent, and later in the year, following a paper by his employer on "the arrangement of the organs of the human head", contributed to that discussion too. By January, 1839, he was helping to run the Lyceum's affairs, and in March he gave the second of a series of lectures on "The natural history of fishes and reptiles", which he was asked to complete at later meetings. The *Doncaster Gazette*, which reported regularly on the activities of the Lyceum, pronounced that the audience for Lankester's talk was "numerous and highly respectable", and that the lecture itself, on the beauty of the adaptation of frogs to their environment, was given in "a most amusing manner". This was the first of many complimentary comments on Lankester's lecturing style which recurred throughout his life.

In July, 1838, the indefatigable Wood family decided to bring culture to the village itself by joining with others to form the somewhat awkwardly named Campsall Society for the Acquisition of Knowledge of Campsall Sunday School, and Lankester was one of those who addressed teachers and friends from the surrounding villages at the opening ceremony, as well as on other occasions. The Society was endowed with a library of some 300 volumes, of which some were given by the reclusive Mrs Wood.[3] Its Vice-President was a well-loved public figure, Dr. Edward Scholfield, who was also a doyen of the Doncaster Lyceum. Lankester must have come to know him well, for a few years later he dedicated his second book to him "as a testimony of my sincere respect for your professional talents and moral excellence ... as well as the kindness with which you have assisted me in collecting many of the materials".[4]

This little book of 151 pages has the very comprehensive title, *An Account of Askern and its Mineral Springs, together with a Sketch of the Natural History and a brief Topography of the Immediate Neighbourhood*. Though for various reasons its publication was delayed until 1842, it was, in fact, the first fruit of that fascination with natural history which Lankester had originally shown at Saffron Walden. Askern was a village in the parish of Campsall which was well known locally for its mineral springs, and Lankester became deeply interested, not only in the quality of the water, but in the geology of the district and the flora and fauna associated with it: throughout his scientific and medical writings there are occasional references to Askern. His book begins with a geological map and a description of Campsall and Askern villages and their amenities. He and his friend Dr. Schmitz, the Woods' German tutor, even "made some search with a spade" in a local archeological site, but could deduce nothing from their efforts. There follow detailed sections on the geology, botany and zoology of the district including comments on the beauty of the (named) larger fungi, which he regarded as a highly interesting but much neglected group. The second section of the book is devoted to a chemical analysis of the spring water carried out by himself with the aid of a skilled assistant. The results were chiefly notable for the high content of hydrogen sulphide, and Lankester concludes the book with sections on the properties of the water and instructions for its use. He was to retain an interest in the composition and content of waters throughout his medical career.

Dr. Leonard Schmitz, Ll.D. (1807-1890), who had helped him with his archeological dig, and with whom he formed a lifelong friendship, had only joined the Wood ménage a few months before Lankester. He had been born near Aix-en-Chapelle and graduated in arts subjects from Bonn University in 1833. In 1836 he married a young Englishwoman who was studying German at Bonn, took British nationality, and was appointed as tutor to the Wood family in 1837. From then on he proceeded to an ever more distinguished career in literature and education, both in England and Scotland (a career meriting over two columns in the *Dictionary of National Biography*). Lankester must have prevailed upon this brilliant man to teach him German, and must have acquired a working knowledge of both the spoken and written language in a remarkably short space of time, for there is no other explanation as to how he achieved the next step in his career.

That he was determined to get a University degree there can be no doubt, as he had written to University College almost as soon as he arrived at Campsall for details of the course for the Doctorate of Medicine which had just been inaugurated under the new Charter.[5] But nothing had come of this idea, probably because the course was too long and expensive. In the spring of 1839, however, he packed his bags, travelled to Heidelberg, and enrolled at the Ruprecht-Karls University, presumably having paid off his debts to his friends at Saffron Walden and saved or borrowed enough money for this next enterprise. It was not until 1858 that Heidelberg University had a mandatory four-year residence qualification for its medical graduates; in 1839 it was sufficient for a candidate simply to pass the final examination. Lankester must have spent the next few months practising the German language and working rapidly through those parts of the curriculum not covered in sufficient depth by his course at University College. But that course must have been of a very high standard, for at the end of September he presented himself for examination, sitting written papers in anatomy, physiology, internal medicine, gynaecology and medical chemistry, and writing essays on inguinal hernia, inflammation of the liver and the Caesarian operation. He wrote his papers in English, German and Latin,[6]* an astonishing feat for a 25-year-old whose schooling had ceased at the age of twelve. The oral examination took place on 1st October and he was not kept in suspense for long, for the next day he was awarded the Degree of Doctor of Medicine with Honours.[18] Shortly afterwards he returned to Campsall in triumph and began to consider his future career, but not before entering into a correspondence on poisonous snakes in the *Lancet*.

The following year he apparently made an abortive attempt to settle in Leeds[7] then "somewhat unexpectedly moved to London",[4] where he took up residence at 43, Hart Street, Bloomsbury, and probably attempted to set up in practice. Why he made such a sudden move is unclear, as he had not been offered salaried employment. He did, however, perhaps through Lindley, assume almost immediately the honourary position of Secretary to Section D (Botany and Zoology) of the British Association for the Advancement of Science, an organisation which had come into being only nine years earlier. Lankester held the secretaryship for 22 years and his work for the Association will be chronicled more fully later (Chapter 4). Though the post did nothing to solve his financial problems, it must have been of the utmost importance in his future career, for through it he made the acquaintance of a large circle of influential people. It was at this time that he came to know Edward Forbes the brilliant young zoologist whose home he later shared, Arthur Henfrey, the botanist and, outside the field of science, Charles Dickens and many others. Lankester's obituarists unanimously remark on his genial and friendly nature, and this trait would have served in good stead the son of a poverty stricken widow from the provinces trying to find his feet in the scientific and literary world of London.

It seems that for the next few years Lankester managed to survive in London largely through lecturing on scientific and medical subjects to a wide variety of audiences, and through writing articles and reviews for the scientific and literary press, doubtless having obtained the initial introductions through his various influential friends. He earned little from his medical practice at this or any other time, and ceased to practise altogether in 1862. As a lecturer, however, he became much sought after. The *Medical Times and Gazette* commented: "Without any profundity of knowledge ... by a happy readiness of expression, a good delivery and a fine presence, [he succeeded] to obtain a great reputation as a popular lecturer"[8]. Time and time again contemporaries made similar remarks, though reading verbatim reports of some of his lectures and scientific

---

* After completing the research for this study, I discovered R. E. W. Sillett's (1956) biographical thesis on Lankester.[6] I have acknowledged the source of the few facts which were new to me, but on a number of others I find myself in disagreement.

papers today, one would consider them very rambling and wordy. His literary efforts included numerous articles for the *Daily News*, some of them on medical reform,[9] and for the *Athenaeum*. He contributed to the latter all through his life, but claimed particularly[1] that up to 1849 he was responsible with few exceptions for all the critical articles on medicine, dietetics, sanitary reform, physiology and natural history.* He also wrote, from 1841, "the greater part of the articles on Botany, Medicine and Physiology in the *Penny Cyclopaedia* from the letter R [where he took over from Professor Lindley] to the end of the work, and also the Supplement"[1] and rewrote these articles in abridged form for the *National Cyclopaedia*. The *Penny Cyclopaedia*, which had been appearing in penny parts since 1833, was an influential and popular work to which his friend Dr. Schmitz also contributed.

Despite his major concern with botany and popular science over this period, it is clear that Lankester's primary intention was still to settle down as a doctor in private practice, but patients were not flocking to his door despite his influential friends. Indeed, in London he could not expect to attract the wealthier citizens unless he could prove himself their social equal by qualifying as a physician. This he was now, in theory at least, in a position to do, for was he not a graduate of a respected European university? The Royal College of Physicians, however, was very jealous of its monopoly, and especially grudging of its licences to practice in London, where too much competition could reduce its Fellows' income. Consequently it offered two types of licence - the Extra-Licence, which entitled the holder to practice as a physician in the provinces after passing an examination; and the full Licence, which granted practice in London after a second examination. That is, Londoners merited physicians of a higher calibre than inhabitants of the provinces.

Lankester must have started to work for the Extra-Licence almost as soon as he arrived in London, for in January, 1841, he produced for the College his Degree Diploma from Heidelberg and his Certificates of Honorable Distinction, medical studies and hospital attendance from University College, sat the examination, and was granted the Extra-Licence to practice outside London.[10] No sooner had he obtained it than he applied for the post of Resident Medical Officer at the recently opened University College Hospital and, on the strength of his good results in the London examinations, was accepted and served for five months.[1]

It was not until the following year, when Lankester was 28 years old, that he attained a reasonably assured and regular source of income, though even then it was probably not sufficient to live on unless augmented by lecturing and writing. First he was appointed Lecturer in

---

* It is not possible to check this, as most reviews in the *Athenaeum* are unsigned.

Materia Medica at the School of Medicine, Grosvenor Place. This establishment, known later as St. George's School, Grosvenor Place, and finally simply as Grosvenor Place School of Medicine and Anatomy, was one of the most illustrious private medical schools in London. It had been founded in 1830 by a great demonstrator in anatomy, Samuel Lane, to act as an anatomy school for the adjacent St. George's Hospital. Lane was unpopular with the medical staff of the Hospital, and a few years later they opened their own rival school nearby. But its staff were not as distinguished as those of the Grosvenor Place School of Medicine and Anatomy which had no trouble, not only in holding its own, but in expanding until it could offer a complete range of subjects.[11] Lankester did well to be accepted on to the staff of such an august establishment. He held the part-time post until 1858, when his resignation may have been due to his becoming Superintendant of the Food Museum at South Kensington (Chapter 10).

In the same year that he obtained the lectureship at the Grosvenor Place School he was appointed to another part-time post, that of Physician (promoted to Senior Physician in 1845[12]) to Farringdon General Dispensary, situated at 17, Bartlett's Buildings, Holborn, and this despite the fact that he only held the Extra-Licence of the College of Physicians. The dispensaries were entirely out-patient institutions, so they were very cheap to run compared with in-patient hospitals. The first had been founded in the eighteenth century as charitable institutions, the physicians' appointments were honorary, and the sick poor were treated free of charge. But during the 1820s provident dispensaries, to which the poor paid small, regular contributions and were then entitled to free treatment, were started in the Midlands. This idea spread, and many free dispensaries began to change over to the provident system, in which doctors were paid a small fee in proportion to the number of patients they saw. Out-patient departments at hospitals barely existed at the time, so the poor, who could not afford a doctor, had only the dispensary to turn to, except in cases of major illness and in times of epidemic. As hospitals began to open their own comprehensive out-patients' departments in the early twentieth century, the need for dispensaries fell away and they began to close down.

The Farringdon Dispensary was founded in 1828, and it is known that in 1890 it worked under the provident system: whether it did so in Lankester's time is uncertain. Though the payment under the system was never large, for a struggling doctor it could be important, but even if the Farringdon was a charitable institution in his time, he would have benefitted in two ways from the appointment. First, there was the prestige which the post itself bestowed, less than that in a teaching, or even a large non-teaching, hospital, but nevertheless useful. Secondly there was the experience he would gain. The Farringdon was unusual in London in that it not only provided medical, dental and surgical care, but it was also a lying-in dispensary, that is, it provided midwives who would deliver women in their own homes. So its doctors would see, for the first time, the whole hideous spectrum of disease among the poor. But more important than the patients they saw on the premises in opening their eyes to the plight of the cities' poor was the requirement to visit the homes of those too sick to travel. For many a physician whose only experience outside his salubrious private practice was in a hospital, what he found during his excursions into territory quite unknown to him was not only horrifying and alarming, but excited his pity and his determination to try to alleviate the conditions that brought his fellow men so low. It could well have been his experience as a dispensary physician that was one of the important factors in shaping Lankester's career.[13,14]

It was not until he had been at the Dispensary for a year, flouting the rules of the Royal College of Physicians, that that establishment decided to act. On November 24, 1843, "the Board having been informed that ... Dr. Edwin Lankester [was] practising as [a] Physician in London having only the Extra-Licence from the College, it has ordered that the usual admonition should be left at his residence by the Bedel".[15] Now, although the Charter of the College stated that only men with a full Licence could practice in London, the Apothecaries' Act of 1815 had, as we have seen, given the Society of Apothecaries the right to examine its Licenciates in the science and practice of medicine and surgery (and later on, midwifery) and so regularized a practice that had been going on for many years. Whatever the College may have wished, case law since then had effectively removed its veto over licenced apothecaries (such as Lankester) acting as physicians in London, or indeed elsewhere. But the College did not give up its privileges without a struggle, and if contraventions of its Charter were brought to its notice it acted as though its powers were still intact. Predictably, therefore, neither its Bedel nor its admonitions seem to have disturbed Lankester in any way, and he continued to practise as Physician to the Dispensary. The lack of a London Licence would certainly, however, debar him from the lucrative posts in the prestigious and exclusive teaching hospitals.[16]

Now, in addition to his regular contributions to the lay press, he began his prolific career of scientific and medical writings on an extraordinarily wide range of subjects. There seemed to be little in biology or medicine which did not attract his interest and comment. He had already published on disease of the hip joint in the *Lancet* in 1836-7; from 1842 he contributed a number of articles to the scientific press, especially the *Annals of Natural History*, on matters as varied as the chemistry of sulphurous waters (a continuation of his study of the Askern spring) and the origin of wood in plants. In some articles, for instance in one entitled, "Lecture on the structure, affinities and medical properties of the natural order Ranunculaceae" in the *Pharmaceutical Journal*, he used his position at the Grosvenor School as a qualification for writing. In 1842, in addition to the *Natural History of Askern*, he produced a book entitled *Lives of Naturalists*[7] of which I have been unable to trace a copy. It may, however, have been the information he collected for the *Lives* which accounts for the correspondence between him and Messrs. George Long and Edward Conoley[17] concerning botanists to be included in a forthcoming *Biographical Dictionary* of which they were the editors.

In his first letter, from 43, Hart Street in October, 1841, Lankester wrote that, at the suggestion of Dr. Schmitz, he was enclosing the names of 18 botanists beginning with A, all foreign and some going back to classical times, which were missing from a list he had seen, and asking if he could supply their biographies. Scribbled across this letter is a note from the recipient, Mr. Long, saying that the offer "is of no use now". However, at Long's request, Lankester wrote again with a list of modern botanists beginning with A, and suggested that he would be happy to undertake, in addition, the notices of many others who had distinguished themselves in the fields of medical botany and natural history. The attempt to obtain additional work was not entirely successful, for Long had already employed a Dr. Paget to deal with the physicians. There followed a series of letters from Lankester enclosing finished notices, discussing others, and making frequent apologies and excuses for delays.

By November, 1842, by which time Lankester had moved house to 19, Golden Square (Chapter 4), the patience of the editors was becoming exhausted, and over the letter bearing the next excuse is scrawled a note from Conoley; "So he has said before: he does not seem able to go our pace". Perhaps this was not surprising considering the many irons Lankester had in the fire at the time, but that would be of little comfort to his editors. Long replied to Conoley: "We must give him time. He is an honest man and knows what he is about. Above all, he is a good tempered man, and I love such people as much as I hate their antipodes." By January, 1843, Conoley was exasperated by yet more delays, and noted that this was not the first time that Lankester had used the excuse of the late arrival of proofs. On 5 April matters seem to have come to a head. Lankester apologised for holding back some proofs while a friend checked dates for him, and an acid note from Conoley stated: "He has had this proof a fortnight and a day." Long's patience, too, was at last exhausted for he added: "Yes, and if I can find anybody else he shall not have the opportunity again." Not until 17 April did Lankester at last "return the proofs and confess my sins." By June, 1844, the work was at last completed and Lankester wrote to the Society for the Diffusion of Useful Knowledge, publishers of the *Biographical Dictionary*, asking when payments to contributors would be made: "I need not say to you that these little matters are sometimes of great importance to literary men." Here the correspondence ends. It provides an interesting insight into his character as seen by others, and also into his dilatory working methods due, not to laziness, but to persistently taking on much more than he could possibly hope to do, a trait which would get him into trouble throughout his life.

Chapter Four

Fellow of the Linnean Society 1841-1845

Lankester was already an active member of the British Association for the Advancement of Science some years before he became the Secretary of Section D (Botany and Zoology) in 1841. He first paid the £1 subscription in 1837, his last year as a student at University College, presumably at the suggestion of Professor Lindley who was Vice-President of the Section at the time.[1] He was joining a very young Association which had been founded at York only six-years earlier by a group of 23 gentlemen scientists whose object was to advance science by the exchange of ideas outside the small circle of Londoners. Knowledge and interest was to be spread to the provinces by co-operation with local philosophical and other societies, so influencing public opinion and hence, the founders hoped, the government. That first meeting at York was a genuine festival of science, and the new Association immediately became "a vehicle of social intercourse, rational amusement, intellectual improvement, personal advertisement and civic pride".[2] The founder members were almost all graduates, members of the Church of England (a number were ordained) and interested primarily in the physical sciences. They believed firmly in the existing social order and urged that the humbler classes should be treated with respect but should on no account be encouraged to cross the social divide. Despite this, from very early on a popular lecture was given at each annual meeting and drew huge and enthusiastic audiences from the working classes.

There were two classes of membership, Life, paid by the gentlemen scientists and their aristocratic supporters, and Annual, paid by the less well off and by the local worthies of the city in which the Association was meeting. The latter, who included shop-keepers and tradesmen, rather diluted the social and scientific respectability of the Association, but their financial contributions were useful. However, in order to keep the meetings as exclusive as possible, an admission charge was instituted in 1840, thus favouring the "well bred, well heeled gentlemen at the expense of the earnest but less well endowed".[2]

Such was the calibre of the audience to which Lankester read his first two papers to the Association at the Birmingham meeting of 1839, one "On the formation of woody tissue" (on which his subsequent article in the *Annals of Natural History* was based[3]), and the other on some abnormal white bream from Campsall. This was followed by a demonstration of a technique for the preservation of fish for display in museums, foreshadowing his future interest in those institutions. In the paper on woody tissue he set out to dispute the theory of a M. Du Petit Thuars that woody fibres are formed by buds and leaves and sent down the stem by them, between the bark and the mature wood, where they are nourished by the cambium. Lankester cited a number of common observations, for instance, that woody tissue is found in leafless plants such as *Monotropa*, and that tree wounds heal from the lower as well as from the upper lip, which would dispose of this theory. He also noted that healing in a ringing experiment which he himself had carried out on beech trees gave a similar result.[4]

At this meeting, Edward Forbes (1815-1854) (Fig. 8), the brilliant young Scottish naturalist, began his short Secretaryship of Section D, and it must have been here that he and Lankester cemented their friendship. Forbes had started to study for a medical degree in Edinburgh, but had taken a dislike to the subject and left the University in 1836. He was fascinated by living things, was a superb experimentalist, and is best known now for his studies of marine fauna, both living and fossil, in the search for which he raised the finance for exploration and dredging expeditions at the same time as earning his living as Professor of Botany at King's College, London, and in other teaching posts. He was a rare character with boundless energy, who loved social life, hated pomp and snobbery, saw only the good in his fellow men, and had a unique and all-pervasive sense of humour.

It was Forbes's dislike of snobbery which led him to found the famous Red Lion Club, of which Lankester was an original member, at the Birmingham meeting of the British Association. The support of the aristocracy, and indeed of royalty, was deemed essential to the prestige of the Association, so suitable entertainment had to be provided for them. This evolved into a peculiarly lavish style of feasting which, "though there was some danger that the members would be rendered *hors de combat* by indigestion, it was generally agreed that the risk was worth taking".[2] Professor Sedgwick, the geologist, remarked in 1837: "Were ever philosophers so fed before? Twenty hundredweight of turtle were sent to fructify in the hungry stomachs of the sons of science!".[2] In addition to the Association Dinner there was a round of private dinners and house-parties. Clearly only the select few could afford entertainment on this scale; the younger scientists, struggling to make their names, were excluded. So Forbes stepped in.

Fig. 8. Edward Forbes, aged 34.

At the Birmingham meeting he had already established himself at the Red Lion public house where a group of other young and high-spirited scientists joined him, forming themselves into the Red Lion Club presided over by the Lion King and the Lion Chaplain who, for grace, intoned, "Brother Lions, let us prey". The waiters' ministrations and the members' speeches were greeted by growls, roars and the wagging of coat-tails rather than by thanks or applause. The Club met for many years during the Annual Association meetings, one of its highlights being the humorous songs composed by Forbes on some scientific subject and sung after the Dinner. In 1844 the London members, undoubtedly including Lankester who had been sharing a house in Golden Square with Forbes for the last two years, combined to set up a dining club, the Metropolitan Red Lion Association, complete with a crest, a red lion regardant holding a tankard in one paw and a church-warden pipe in the other. The Lion King wore a velvet cap emblazoned with red lions rampant, and invitations to meetings read: "Feeding of the Carnivores, six o'clock precisely".[5]

Meanwhile Professor Lindley, still bent on promoting Lankester's botanical career, stepped in again, this time to propose him for Fellowship of the Linnean Society, Britain's oldest and most prestigious natural history society. It had been founded in 1788 by a group of naturalists headed by a Scot, James Edward Smith, to provide suitable premises to house an extremely valuable collection of the manuscripts, books and specimens of the great Carl Linneaus which Smith had purchased while still a student. But there were many delays, the Society became moribund, and it was not until after Smith's death in 1828 that it was able to buy the collection for itself, and then began slowly to revive. It had still not quite regained its first promise when Lankester was proposed for fellowship in 1840, but by 1858 its prestige was such that it was able to move into its present headquarters in the entrance arch of Burlington House, Piccadilly.[6]

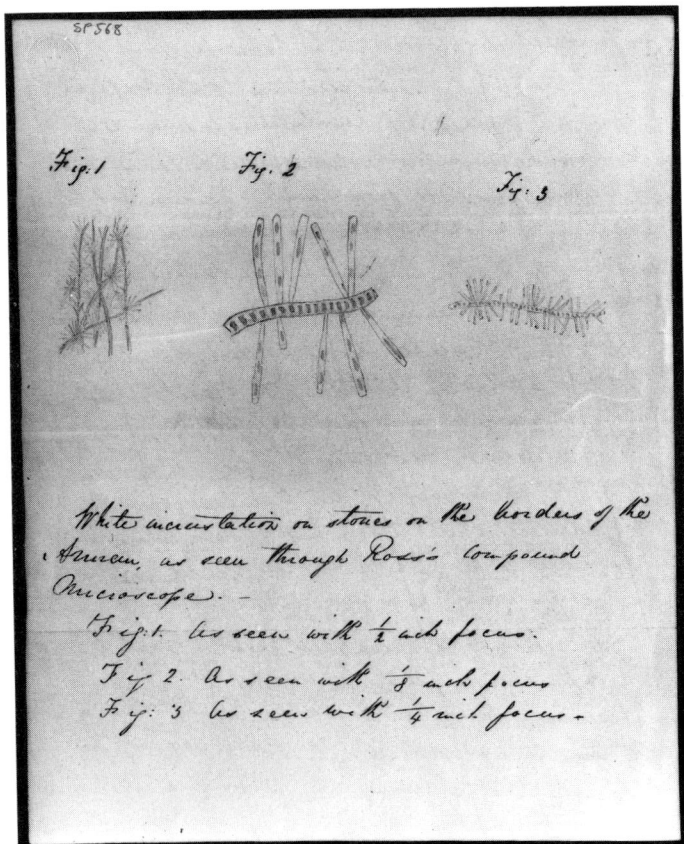

Fig. 9. Page from the manuscript of Edwin Lankester's paper on *Synedra ulna*.

To support his proposal, Lindley chose Nathaniel Ward, the inventor of the Wardian Case (the progenitor of the modern bottle garden) with whom he was campaigning for the removal of excise duties on glass which were proving very damaging to the horticultural industry,[7] George Bentham, his colleague at the Royal Horticultural Society, and two other biologists. On 7th March, 1840, "Edwin Lankester of Campsall Hall" (an address which gives a highly misleading impression of both his social and financial standing), "a gentleman well acquainted with Botany and other branches of Natural History", was elected. In the year of his election he read a paper on an infusorium, *Synedra ulna**, which had been named only two years earlier, and which he had found growing on a submerged stone in the River Annan. The paper was illustrated with line drawings (Fig. 9)[8,9]. As the British Association had met in Glasgow that year, it is likely that Lankester had taken advantage of the occasion to make a field trip during which he collected the organisms. He was not a very active member of the Society. Apart from contributing a Short Communication in each of the years 1844 and 1845 he took no further part in its proceedings until 1850, when he was elected to its Council and delivered a paper on "A peculiar structure of the cells of the surface of *Callitriche nema*".[10] During his year on Council he attended most of its meetings, together with the Society's general meetings, but after 1852 his name ceases to appear in the General Minute Book and two years later he had to be reminded not only once, but twice, to pay his subscription.

In contrast to his slight participation in Linnean Society affairs, he remained a lively member of the British Association for many years. At the Plymouth meeting in 1841 he followed his papers at York with another report on his natural history researches at Campsall, and at Manchester in the following year he gave an expanded account of the infusoria he had found in Scottish and other waters and had reported on briefly at the Linnean. It was at Manchester too that he accepted the honorary post of Secretary to Section D (Botany and Zoology), a position which he would fill for the next 22 years. Not all the work would fall on his shoulders, however, for each year from one to three other secretaries were appointed to help him, usually including local members from the town in which the Association would be meeting that year; but Lankester was in overall charge of the organization of the Section, including arrangements for the speakers and the programme.[11]

Through the Secretaryship he was drawn into many other aspects of the Association's affairs. In 1842 he sat on two committees. One, which included Sir Richard Owen, zoologist, and Charles Babington, botanist, among its members, was charged with obtaining information regarding

---

* Now accepted as a diatom

the "varieties of the human race", for which it had the sum of £5 at its disposal. It continued its investigations until 1844 when a new committee was set up to investigate the "Periodical phaenomena of animals and vegetables". Again, Owen and Babington were among the ten members, Forbes also joined it, and Lankester himself held the £10 grant. The idea stemmed from the work of a Belgian naturalist who was making a systematic study of the correlation between the timing of regular phenomena in living organisms, such as bud burst and leaf fall in plants, or the first appearance of migrant birds, and seasonal changes in temperature, pressure, moisture, sunlight, etc. It was felt that if scientific records could be kept on selected species for a number of years and over a wide area they might yield interesting results. The Committee produced instructions for the participants, together with standard forms which were to be filled in, and each year afterwards, but on a reduced grant of £5, the Committee met and tables of results were published. By 1853 the Committee had dwindled to three, including Lankester and Owen, and 1857 is the last year in which it is mentioned in the Association's *Reports*. Lankester then laid some completed forms on the table, complaining that every year many were taken but few filled in, and read a paper based on theories totally at variance with those accepted today.

In most years up to 1850 he read papers on a wide variety of subjects, often more than one at a single meeting. They ranged from those already recorded to a discussion on the chemistry of germination, descriptions of plants of possible economic use, and plant "monstrosities" as illustrations of the laws of morphology. His interests were wide; he became fascinated for a short while by each new subject he came across but seldom concentrated on one for long enough to obtain any deep insight into it. That he thoroughly enjoyed the Association's annual assemblies is shown by an aside in a business letter to Sir William Jardine (see below) in 1846: "We had a capital Section D at Southampton especially Zoology, and of course the Red Lions flourished accordingly.[12]

During the York meeting of 1844 a new society composed of some of the Association's members held its first meeting. In the words of its Secretary, Dr. Edwin Lankester, the Ray Society had its origin in a wish, expressed by Dr. Johnston of Berwick to some of his scientific friends, that some means might be devised "for printing such works on Natural History as stand in need of extraneous assistance to ensure their publication". Lankester went on to describe the extreme difficulty of obtaining financial backing for this purpose from the government, or even from the British Association whose funds were inadequate. Thus much original work of great scientific import never saw the light of day.

To rescue such precious materials from oblivion is one of the objects for which the Ray Society was instituted, and it has been ascertained that by applying the whole funds of the Society ... to the printing and issuing of appropriate volumes ... a large dividend of scientific matter may be annually distributed to the subscribers.

The Society would also undertake the editing, translation and reprinting of rare or inaccessible works.[13]

Dr. Johnston, whose idea the new Society was, was a marine biologist and a pillar of the Berwick Naturalists' Club. He had discussed his idea with the President of the British Association the previous year, and had received enough support by February, 1844, to announce the founding of the Ray Society with a nucleus of active members from the British Association which included not only Lankester, but Forbes and Owen. The subscription was fixed at one guinea, and by the time of the York meeting there were over 400 members. The decision to call the new Society after the great seventeenth century clergyman and universal naturalist was a brilliant one. John Ray (1627-1705) had spent his life in a passionate exploration of every branch of natural history, from fossils to flowers, fish and mammals, and from comparative anatomy to the functions of the living organism. The results of his wide-ranging but detailed observations led him to a reasoned system of classification which greatly benefitted the later work of Carl Linneus.

One of the founder members of the Ray Society was Sir William Jardine (1800-1874), seventh baronet of Applegirth, Dumfriesshire, a devoted ornithologist and fellow member with Johnston of the Berwick Naturalists. It is thanks to Sir William's membership of the Council of the newly founded Ray Society, and his inability because of his geographic isolation to attend many meetings thereof, that we have some insight into the proceedings of that body; for it was the duty of the Secretary to keep him informed of events, and Lankester's letters are still among Jardine's papers. Council meetings were usually held at Lankester's home, for a hand-written notice informed Jardine that a meeting would be held at 4pm on 2nd May, 1840, at 19, Golden Square: and later, after Lankester had moved to 22, Old Burlington Street, this is also given as the Society's address. Jardine did not attend the Council Meeting of 2nd May, and a few days later Lankester wrote to him about three of the matters discussed. Forbes had proposed that their first volume should consist of a selection of foreign reports on recent progress in botany and zoology, but the motion had not been put. Then two propositions for consideration at the next meeting had been carried: that either some of the work of Ray, or an *Iconographia Linnaeanana* should be published. At the next meeting there had been some disagreement, for Lankester reported that most

Counsellors considered that the publication of a series of pamphlets would be the best way to proceed, but that he, Lankester, like Jardine, would prefer to issue volumes. Meanwhile a network of local secretaries was being set up round the country, and membership was increasing. Despite the fact that Forbes's motion of May was not put, it is plain that by July some translations of foreign progress reports were going ahead, for the following year the Society published Lankester's translation from the German of H. F. Link's *Report on the Progress of Physiological Botany during the year 1841*. The corespondence in July was all concerned with the cost of publishing and the choice of publishers, in particular, whether an English or a Scottish publisher should be used. That month the counsellors also made a pilgrimage to Ray's grave at Black Notley, in Essex, but the letter describing the expedition has not survived. By the end of August, Lankester wrote that his translation of Link was almost completed, that they had found "a very nice head of Ray" for the title page and that a "Life and letters of Ray" was being recommended as their second publication, though they had yet to find an editor for it.

On 15th November he passed on to Jardine a severe reprimand from the Council. Jardine had been supervising the translation from the German by a layman of a zoological report, and had been expected to correct the technical errors which would inevitably result before despatching it south. Jardine had apparently supposed that Lankester's duties as Secretary included those of general editor and that it was he who should have been responsible for the corrections. Lankester indignantly repudiated this definition of his responsibilities and continued that "the Council on account of the great errors which exist in the [illegible] forwarded ... have ordered that the whole of the copies of [the] translation up to the present should be cancelled". After this there are only two more letters in the series. One in 1845, was still rather stiff, and explained that the Society had decided not to use Jardine's Scottish publishers for reasons of convenience; and the last, in 1846, reverted once again to the high cost of errors in translation, but ended chattily enough.

In his report to the first (York) meeting of the Society[13], Lankester regretted that it had proved impossible to produce their first volumes (his own translation of Link, and the zoological report which had caused so much friction with Jardine) in time for it, as had been hoped, but announced that they were expected to appear in a few months. Then he listed the Council's proposals for the next three volumes, the first of which was to be the *Memorials of John Ray*. This was, in fact, the "Life and Latters" previously mentioned for which no editor had been found. Now it had been decided that Lankester himself should edit it, and the book duly appeared in 1845 with, as frontispiece, a beautiful drawing by Edward Forbes of Ray's grave at Black Notley, perhaps done during the Council's

Fig. 10. The tomb of John Ray at Black Notley Church, drawn by Edward Forbes. From *The Memorials of John Ray* edited by Edwin Lankester.

visit there the previous year (Fig. 10). A contemporary review complained that merely republishing the remaining "scattered materials".of Ray's life in no way replaced the need for a proper biography in which his position as a natural scientist was fully developed and discussed;[14] and Ray's biographer, C. E. Raven, a hundred years later was extremely critical of Lankester's editorship, stating that the letters were printed in the wrong order because Lankester did not realize that they were dated in the old style and that the footnotes were usually, and often grossly, misleading.[15] Among four other suggestions for future publications made in the Secretary's report was a translation from the German of Schleiden's *Principles of Scientific Botany*, and this too, in due course, Lankester would undertake. The Ray Society, which is still publishing today, has kept no archives, and I have been unable to discover the duration of Lankester's secretaryship.

Some years prior to 1845 he had given a course of lectures on the natural history of plants yielding food at the Manchester Royal Institute, which had been published in its journal, and in 1845 these were republished under the lengthy title of *Report of Lectures on the Natural History of Plants Yielding Food, with Incidental Remarks on the Functions and Disorders of the Digestive Organs*, to serve as an outline of his course on materia medica at the Grosvenor Place School. In direct contrast to his "Essay on the uncertainty of medical science" in 1836, these lectures show a marked deference towards the Almighty and accept his interference in the affairs of man. For instance:

> A wise and beneficent Creator had abundantly provided more than sufficient for the support of the whole animal kingdom; and whenever the cry of distress was heard, and want of food was its cause, we should remember that some great law of Providence had been broken somewhere.

He continued his emphasis on man's greed as the cause of hunger when he made the plea, still so relevant today, that research should not always be conducted with monetary ends in view, but for the good of "the one great whole".

Lankester's concern that everyone, whatever his or her income, should have access to an adequate food supply, is shown again in a book on a topic closely related to the above, *Vegetable Substances used for the Food of Man*, which first appeared in the Library of Entertaining Knowledge in 1844 and was revised in 1846. In the Introduction he stated that his object was to trace the progress of the country towards "obtaining an abundance and a variety of wholesome and agreeable vegetable food at the cheapest rate and with unfailing regularity for increasing inhabitants", while conceding that in practice, progress towards this aim was not due to soundness of legislation or the foresight of wise politicians, but to a spirit of free commerce. The book is both fuller and more popularly written than his lectures for the Grosvenor Place School, and examines almost every plant of which any part is edible by man, from wheat to breadfruit and from rhubarb to tea.

Towards the end of 1844 Lankester moved from Forbes's home in Golden Square to 22, Old Burlington Street, the only one of his four homes in Westminster still standing. It is a very plain, semi-detatched, 4-storeyed house of brick, its severity only relieved by a row of attic windows and a narrow stone canopy over the front door. There was purpose behind this move, for on 3rd July, 1845, Dr. Edwin Lankester, now aged 31, married

20-year old Miss Phebe Pope, and it was here that they first set up house together. Phebe was the daughter of Samuel Pope and his wife Phebe, née Rushton, of 2, Barnsbury Street, Highbury, a middle class residential suburb which had sprung up on the played-out brickfields of Islington. At that time its population consisted of prosperous tradesmen, minor professional men and private school proprietors. Pope, a former mill-owner from Manchester* described somewhat vaguely on his daughter's marriage certificate as an "Agent", would presumably have been one of the prosperous tradesmen, but his home does not suggest any great wealth, being a very narrow 3-storeyed, terraced house in yellow brick, with attic and basement, and lacking a porch or any adornment whatsoever.

The Pope family were Baptists, for the wedding took place at Islington Green Baptist Church, a plain, red brick building in Providence Place, close to Barnsbury Street**. Whether the couple attended Baptist or Congregational services after the wedding is not known, but as both were Dissenters, religious problems between them would have been unlikely. The witnesses to the marriage were a lawyer, William Smith, and Phebe's brother, Samuel, who would later become a Queen's Counsel.[16]

As to the couple themselves, nothing is known of their first meeting or courtship, but Edwin was a singularly attractive man of whom Phebe could be proud. He is described as "above average height and somewhat portly, with a ruddy complexion and dark brown hair and eyes. His engaging voice and manner accompanied a natural kindness of heart which rendered it impossible for him to be harsh or unjust".[17] Phebe, as her later life showed, was a thoughtful and unconventional young lady with strongly held views. The two may well have been drawn together by their common interest in the plant world, for Phebe was soon to become a capable botanist in her own right. Again, Edwin's views on the education of girls and the place of women in society were, as we shall see, ahead of his time, and this liberal outlook may well have appealed to Phebe, for later in her life she was to devote much time and thought to the welfare and advancement of her sex. She did not, however, neglect the more

---

* Some notes found with Phebe's portrait in Ipswich Museum claim that she was a member of the "well-known Pope family of Suffolk". However, the entry in the *Dictionary of National Biography* for her brother, Samuel Pope (1826-1900), the parliamentary lawyer, states that his father was Samuel Pope of Manchester and that his mother's maiden name was Rushton. As the Lankesters christened one of their sons Rushton, there can be little doubt that Phebe was a Manchester, rather than a Suffolk, Pope.
** The Chapel is now a disused clothing factory, hemmed in by more recent building and huge modern flats.

Fig. 11. *Lankesteria parviflora* (Lindley).

traditional duties of the Victorian wife, for the Lankesters were to have 11 children, seven of whom survived.

The year 1845 saw one other notable event in Edwin's career, for on 18th December he was elected a Fellow of the Royal Society on the grounds that he was "distinguished for his acquaintance with the science of Natural History" and had a number of publications on the subject to his name. Once again Professor Lindley headed the list of his proposers, followed by Richard Owen and eleven others including Edward Forbes.[3] There is no record that he ever took any part in the Society's affairs.

The following year Lindley re-emphasized his high regard for his former pupil when he named after him a new genus, *Lankesteria*, to cover two recently discovered tropical plants, *L. parviflora* and *L. longiflora*, belonging to the Order Acanthaceae. *L. parviflora* (Fig. 11) has tufts of pretty, bright yellow flowers and was recommended for bringing colour to the stove (greenhouse) in winter. In his dedication Lindley said of Lankester that he was "a gentleman whose knowledge of botanical science requires no eulogy".[18] It must have been a disappointment to Lindley when, in a few years' time and before he could become in any way an eminent botanist, it became clear that, of the two careers Lankester could have followed, he had chosen medicine, though he always retained a passionate interest in natural history and especially botany.

Chapter Five

Thwarted Physician   1846-1853

The next few years must have been difficult ones for the Lankesters and deeply frustrating for Edwin. Their eldest child, Fay, had been born in 1846, but their only sources of income, apart from Edwin's books and casual lectures, were his never very lucrative private practice and his part-time posts at the Grosvenor Place School and the Farringdon Dispensary. It was probably as much his financial situation as professional ambition which precipitated his decision to sit for the London Licence of the Royal College of Physicians five years after he had obtained the Extra-Licence.

He submitted himself in September, 1846, was examined "in Parte Physiologica", and told to return a few days later for the second examination. He was then examined "in Parte Pathologica but was not approved".[1] The *Annals* of the College do not give reasons for the failure of candidates, but the result would have come as a severe shock to a man as experienced and highly qualified as Lankester. In the event he was not only shocked, he was extremely angry, and regardless of any future consequences, promptly published a pamphlet stating forthrightly exactly what he thought about the College and its examiners. It is thanks to a Dr. Edward Crisp that we know of this pamphlet, for on reading Lankester's obituaries following his death in 1874, Crisp wrote to the *British Medical Journal*[2] quoting a copy which he had in his possession. In it Lankester said that as he was already a licenciate, he expected to be called upon to answer practical questions, not the sort of question a crammer would pump into a schoolboy. He also mentioned that one of his examiners had, a few years earlier, given him a testimonial for the post at the Farringdon Dispensary which included the words, "I can fully testify to his competency to fill the office ... with credit to himself and much advantage to the objects of the Institution". Another examiner, he noted, was a rival lecturer on materia medica. Dr. Crisp then went on to quote verbatim from the pamphlet:

> If I were a young man who had only had the five years' study which the College requires, I might have, consistently, been sent back for a year; but what must be thought of the value of the College examination which supposes that, the knowledge it requires may be got up in twelve months,

but could not be gained by 18 years of hard study and diligent observations?

At the same time, however, I am not ignorant of the facts that there are gentlemen in London who, in less than a year, would engage to prepare me - as they have done hundreds of other members of the College - in such a manner as to ensure my passing their examination. I have never, however, condescended to the practice of cramming in the four examinations that I have previously submitted to and passed.

I conscientiously regard myself at this moment as fitted to practise my profession: and if the College examinations are of a nature rather to beat the schoolboys' qualifications which may be got up by a cram, than those which have been gained by reading and experience at the bedside, I can only express my regret that the public confidence should have been given to examinations which every member of the College must feel are not worthy of it.

Dr. Crisp ended his letter:

Believing, Sir, that this rejection at the London College of Physicians had much influence on his [Lankester's] later life, and believing also that his rejection under the cirumstances rebounded rather to his credit than his disgrace, I ask you to insert this letter ...

There is no doubt that, as Dr. Crisp said, this was the crisis and turning point of Lankester's career. His private practice could never prosper now, and his chances of obtaining one of the much sought after posts in a voluntary or teaching hospital, which alone could have set him on the path to a consultancy, respectability and financial security, were slim indeed. Many of these posts were in the gift of existing consultants or established medical families, and there was no Professor Lindley among them to smooth Lankester's path to the medical heights: without his London Licence his chances of gaining a hospital post by competition were virtually non-existant. Although he must have known this he still applied, in 1849, for the post of Physician at St. Mary's Hospital, Paddington, and was duly turned down. Dr. Crisp remarked, à propos of his being "shut out" from that post: "this, according to the orthodox system of election, after his rejection at the London College of Physicians, was a matter of course".[2]

Lankester's hopes would have been considerably higher when the Chair of Materia Medica and Therapeutics at his old College fell vacant a little later in the year, for he had by then been teaching materia medica at the Grosvenor Place School for seven years. He applied for the post on 2nd August, and not only have his application and curriculum vitae survived, but so also has the assessors' report to Senate on the applicants[3]. Lankester's application is not one to inspire the confidence of the assessors. It is wordy, as is so much of his writing, and he used a great deal of space explaining away weaknesses in his qualifications and experience rather than enlarging on their strengths. For instance, he apologised for not obtaining more prizes as a student, but made no special mention of the Lindley Prize, surely relevant to a Chair of Materia Medica: and he gave no details of his course in the subject at the Grosvenor Place School until the very end of the application, when he mentioned as an afterthought that he had amassed a good collection of teaching specimens: he listed all his numerous publications and then apologised for their not being immediately concerned with materia medica and therapeutics due to "accidental circumstances". Instead of outlining his attitude to his profession, both to his patients and to medical science, he referred his readers to his "Essay on the Uncertainties of Medical Science". He supplied 13 testimonials from teachers, colleagues and friends (these are lost) including the renowned Samuel Lane, the proprietor of the Grosvenor Place School; John Balfour, Professor of Botany at Edinburgh; Edward Forbes, Richard Owen and Lyon Playfair, who would later play so large a part in government education policy. Lindley was away when the Appointments Committee sat, but he wrote to it on Lankester's behalf.

Two days after Lankester applied for the Chair, he wrote again saying that it had just been brought to his notice that the College would be filling a vacancy for a Physician at the Hospital and he wished to apply. He could add little to what he had said in his application for the Chair except that he had "been to a greater or lesser extent employed in the practise of [his] profession", had taught pupils at the dispensaries at which he was employed (see below), and had lectured in clinical medicine at the Grosvenor Place School in the absence of colleagues. For the rest, he referred the College to its personal knowledge of him as a student and Resident Medical Officer. It does not seem that he took his chances of success very seriously, and one must suppose that his application to St. Mary's had been much more determined. Having done all he could to ensure his future, he went on holiday with Phebe to the Isle of Wight.

From the letters of Charles Dickens, it seems that it was here that the long friendship between the two families began. Dickens was staying at Bonchurch, writing *David Copperfield* in the mornings and devoting the afternoons and evenings to his social life. "There has been", he wrote on 15(?) August to his friend and biographer John Forster[4] "a Dr. Lankester at Sandown, a very good merry fellow, who has made one at the picnics, and whom I went over and dined with, along with Danby, Leach and White". These picnics were a feature of the Dickens family holidays and were often held at Cook's Castle, Shanklin Down. According to Phebe,[5] describing them years later to John Forster, they were organized by the "Sea Serpents" of Bonchurch and the "Red Lions" of Sandown. Though Phebe does not mention her husband it seems inevitable that he must have headed the "Red Lions". Dickens described the picnics:

> On Tuesday we are going on another picnic; with materials for a fire, at my express stipulation; and a great iron pot to boil potatoes in. These things, and the eatables, to go to the ground in a cart.

Awful Appearance of a "Wopps" at a Pic-nic.

Fig. 12. Mr Punch's impression of a Dickens' family picnic at Cook's Castle, Isle of Wight. Guests were present, and the gentleman falling from the barrel may be Edwin Lankester, with Phebe just behind him.

Phebe confirms that Dickens was in charge of boiling the potatoes. Another feature of the picnics was a race over the Downs run by the Dickens's corpulent friend, Mark Lemon, known to the children as "Uncle Porpoise", and the almost equally stout Lankester. Leech, an artist, submitted a lively cartoon of one of these picnics to *Punch*, and on 15 August it duly appeared, entitled "Awful Appearance of a 'Wopps' at a Pic-nic"[6] (Fig. 12). Phebe, writing to Forster in February, 1889, said of this drawing:

> I ought to say perhaps that I cannot identify any of the figures in the Pic-nic [sic] sketch excepting that of C. Dickens himself brandishing a knife, a certain Lord Morben drawing a sword - Mark Lemon tumbling off the hamper, and I believe the pair on the left was intended for me with a parasol and my husband by my side. You see the ruins of Cook's Castle to the right and I remember the exaggerated "Wopps" very vividly.

Three days later she wrote to Forster again:

> ... what I think is the only question is whether the figure tumbling off the hamper was intended for Mark Lemon or for my own husband, Dr. Lankester. The girl on the left holding the parasol is myself.

After their return from holiday the Lankesters had two and a half months to wait for the results of Edwin's job applications.

The Appointments Committee's report on the applicants for the Chair, submitted to Senate on 14 November, was scrupulously fair. Only one candidate other than Lankester was considered, the obviously brilliant Dr A. B. Garrod, who had obtained both his M.B. and M.D. at London University and been awarded a Gold Medal on each occasion. His subsequent papers had reported the results of highly original research which had "extended the limits of chemical and medical science". The assessors filled four and a half manuscript pages with their carefully weighed deliberations, finding Lankester's testimonials particularly impressive. They quoted the letter from the absent Professor Lindley who considered Dr. Garrod's "acquaintance with Natural History to be defective" but found Lankester's notable. The Committee unanimously agreed, too, that Lankester was a far better lecturer than Garrod, who was condemned as "not by any means satisfactory in this regard". Nevertheless, they were convinced that Dr. Garrod possessed "superior powers of mind" and recommended his appointment, though they added a rider that had the Chair been one of materia medica only, and not of therapeutics as well, they were "inclined to believe that Dr. Lankester would have been better qualified to fill it". Finally they attached Professor

Lindley's letter as an appendix to their report, "in which he expresses strongly his preference for Dr. Lankester". The Committee had a difficult choice to make, but it is not surprising that Lankester, with his very average intellect, was outclassed by Garrod's brilliance, even if the students would be condemned to many hours of suffering.

It must have been a devastating moment for Lankester when he learned of his failure to obtain the Chair now that his path to success in medicine was also blocked, and this failure was further reinforced when he was also turned down for the post of Physician at the Hospital, though he would have known that, in the circumstances, this was a foregone conclusion.

One of the facts which he did not mention in his application to University College Hospital was that he was a member of the Westminster Medical Society, and had been active in it for some time. Its *Proceedings*, which were published only from 1848-9, are lost, but some of its activities are recorded in the medical press[7]. The Society had been founded in 1809 and met on Saturday evenings at 17, Savile Row, and it is recorded that Lankester was on its Committee in 1848-9 and was Vice-President with Dr. John Snow (Chapter 6) in 1850, the year in which the Society merged with the Medical Society of London. Over the years 1849-50 Lankester spoke on rupture of the right auricle, the cholera fungus (Chapter 6), a case of cancer of the bladder complicated by fungal growth, fatty kidney, opium poisoning, and a late death from chloroform, a list as varied as his interests in natural history, and presumably mostly cases seen in his Dispensary practice.

However, they were not cases from the Farringdon Dispensary as, for undiscovered reasons, he had ceased to practise there in about 1847. Instead, in 1849 he had obtained the post of Attending Physician at the Royal Pimlico Dispensary and Lying-in Institution which at the time was established at 1, Belgrave Terrace, Buckingham Palace Road, but moved to No. 30 in 1853. From its foundation in 1831 it was a fee-paying organization the charges, probably paid monthly, being: adults, 10d; children under 18, 8d; man, wife and child, 1s 2d; widow, 5d; maternity cases were charged one guinea.[8,9] Lankester would have· been paid according to the number of patients he saw, so it is impossible to assess his income from this source, but his continued direct contact with the plight of London's poor would have reinforced all that he had already seen at the Farringdon. He held the post until 1856, when he probably resigned on taking up wider responsibilities.

It was on 2 June, 1849 that Lankester first entered the public service, initially on a voluntary basis; for on that day he was elected to the Vestry of St. James's, Westminster, the parish in which he lived, "for two years in the room of Mr. George Garrett, appointed to the Office of Churchwarden of the said Parish".[10] The Vestry was the parish assembly of which, in a historical harkback, the vicar and churchwardens were *ex officio* members and whose other members were chosen according to a variety of criteria. By this date there was no religious test for vestrymen, and in the countryside all male ratepayers could attend meetings. In the metropolis,

Fig. 13. The new (1862) Vestry Hall of St. James's Church, Piccadilly, with the church on the left.

which had over 90 parishes, the vestries were "close" or "select" and consisted, according to the size of the parish, of some 30 to 100 "principle inhabitants" (the qualifications for this exalted status varied) who were elected by show of hands by those parishioners who were rated above a certain minimum sum varying from parish to parish. The vestries were nominally overseen by the local Bench, and they dealt with paving, lighting, street cleaning, poor relief and keeping the peace, though over the years their responsibilities grew, particularly in relation to public health. The domain of the vestries overlapped with that of two other important bodies, the Metropolitan Commission for Sewers and the Poor Law Commission, the latter being represented locally by the Board of

Guardians, elected by the ratepayers, which was in overall charge of parish relief. Nominally the Board of Guardians was independent of the vestry, but though the Poor Rate was estimated by the former, it had to be voted in by the latter. The vestrymen themselves were drawn mainly from among the local tradesmen, together with builders and solicitors; their whole object was to keep the rates as low as possible, with the result that they were mean and pennypinching in the extreme and enforced the most stringent and vicious economies. Only a few vestries, such as St. Marylebone, had a large proportion of professional men and aristocrats among their members, and they were usually among the better run. On the whole attendance at vestry meetings was poor; for instance, St. James's, Westminster, had 60 vestrymen of whom only 15 to 18 attended regularly.

St. James's Vestry met at the Vestry Hall which stood in Piccadilly just to the west of St. James's Church*[9] (Figs. 13, 14). There may have been quite a number of professional men in its ranks, for though the parish included some appalling slums, Lankester was by no means the only medical resident, the Westminster Medical Society met there, Burlington House was within its boundaries, and its southern boundary was adjacent to Green Park. It was the smallest of the London parishes, covering only 162 acres (Fig. 14). Why Lankester decided to stand for the vacancy left by Mr. Garrett we cannot now know; he may have been asked to do so, or he may have put himself forward in the belief that he had something to contribute to the welfare of his fellow parishioners, for the record of his contributions to Vestry meetings makes it clear that, true to his nature, he took his duties very seriously, and in his eyes those duties were to improve the lot of the neediest of his fellow men, not to save the ratepayers' money. He was re-elected at the end of his 2-year term and again in 1854 when the normal 3-year term finished, and the Vestry Minutes,[10] written in a magnificent copperplate hand, show that he attended with considerable regularity.

The Minutes are terse, preserving no records of the discussions or their participants, but Lankester took an active part in the proceedings, proposing motions and being appointed to a number of ·committees, including the Public Baths and Wash-Houses Committee. At a Special Meeting on 25 March, 1850, he proposed that the Vestry should order payment from the Poor Rate of the excess needed over the estimate to allow it to carry out its duties under the Public Baths and Wash-Houses

---

* On the site of the present Midland Bank. The original single-storey building, just visible on the extreme left of Fig. 32, was replaced in 1862 by the imposing Hall in Fig. 13.

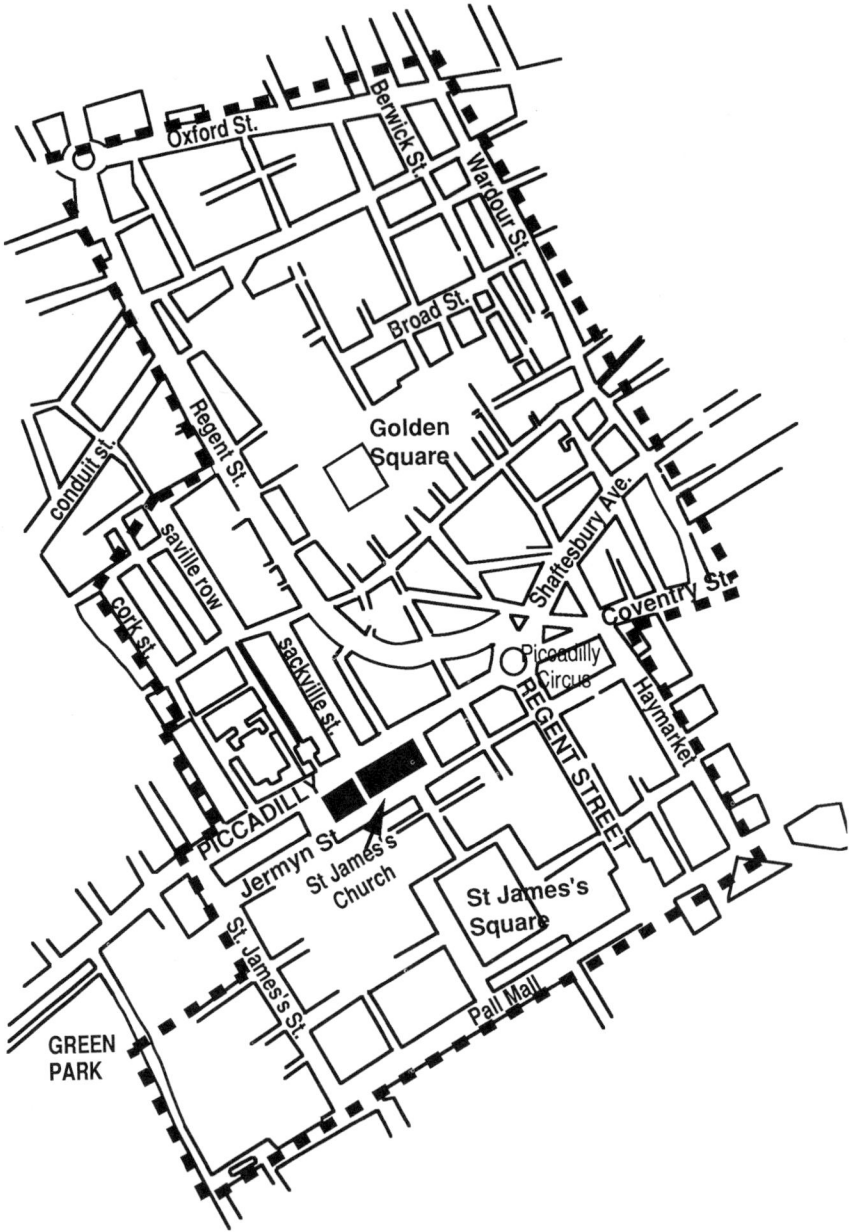

Fig. 14. Map of the parish of St. James's, Westminster. The dotted line marks the parish boundary.

Act. And in May that year, when they were considering the Metropolitan Interments Bill which was being introduced to attack the urgent problem of lack of burial space within parish boundaries for London's exploding population, Lankester proposed that a committee be set up to examine the measure, and was himself elected on to it. After examining the draft Act carefully, the Committee took strong exception to the fact that a body empowered to levy rates, the new Burial Board, would not be accountable to rate-payers. Any new board, they stipulated, must include elected members. After the Act had been passed in 1852, the Vestry became worried about the expense which the new Burial Boards would entail, and decided to discuss with the other Westminster parishes the formation of a joint Board. Lankester headed the deputation appointed to meet the other parishes.

Towards the end of 1851 he found himself on a committee looking into the feasibility of building an artesian well to supply the parish with clean water. The difficulty here seems to have been not so much the will to do the job, as the means. The Paving Committee agreed that it was empowered to finance the well, but not to pipe the water to each house; whereupon the Vestry withdrew its offer of land on which to build the well, whether with relief or disappointment is not stated. No more is heard of the project. In 1853, to add to the variety of his duties, he joined a committee looking into the income of the Rector, the other members of which included the two churchwardens. It reported back in May, but the outcome of its deliberations is not recorded. It is strange to find the Vestry, nominally now a lay body with no allegiance to the Church, investigating such a matter, and even stranger to find Lankester, presumably still a Congregationalist, on the Committee. That he had moved to the Church of England is possible, as he would, in due time, be buried in the graveyard of a parish church: but on the other hand, he had held a Chair at a Congregationalist seminary for some years.

The Lankesters' second child had been born on 15 May, 1847, and named Edwin Ray after the great botanist so revered by his father. Later on this son, as Sir Ray Lankester, would far outshine his father in the world of science and in the public eye. Meanwhile, despite Edwin's efforts, there had been no increase in the family income, and it may have been partly to remedy this that in 1850, having failed to obtain more prestigious posts in either medicine or science, he applied for and obtained the Chair of Natural Sciences at the soon-to-be-opened New College, at a salary of £200 a year. Once again it was a part-time job, and he retained both his other posts. The College building, in Gothic style, stood on the Finchley Road on the slope of Hampstead Hill, and was just being completed; it was opened in 1851 (Fig. 15). New College (which was not a part of the University of London) was the result of the fusion of three colleges for the education of Congregationalist ministers, and for this purpose it was to give a five-year liberal education which would also be open to students not entering the Ministry. Its Faculty of Arts was to include a School of Natural Sciences, and it was of this School that Lankester became the first Professor. The course he gave lasted two years; in the first, the students covered chemistry, mineralogy and geology, which he regarded as essential background for the life sciences; in the second year the curriculum included botany, vegetable physiology, zoology and comparative anatomy.[11] Immediately on his appointment he was allotted £50 for the purchase of specimens and apparatus for his museum and laboratories in preparation for the start of lectures in 1851.[12]

Lankester's Introductory Lecture was, as usual, rather verbose. First he considered the reasons for the inclusion of natural science in a liberal theological education. Its study trains the mind, he said, in a different way from that of mathematics and languages; it instils a habit of observation, it is essential for the maintenance of man's well-being, for the understanding of industry and commerce, and finally, it is "the handmaid of religion" and only by understanding it can theologians defend religion from attack. There was no undue emphasis on religion in the lecture, and where it was mentioned, Lankester's position was the same as that described more fully in a series of lectures he had given to the Young Men's Christian Association a year or two earlier. They were entitled "The Natural History of Creation"[13], and set out the speaker's beliefs about evolution (or Progress, as he termed it), its driving force, direction and purpose, twelve years before the publication of *The Origin of Species*.

His views were strictly anthropocentric. He considered that the history of Creation had been PROGRESS (his emphasis), and that this Progress "had had prospectively in view the welfare and happiness of man". He believed, in addition, that "man's spiritual nature or reason is obedient to the same law of progress, or may be brought under and viewed from the idea of progress". Progress, he said, "is an idea founded on certain facts, by which we may examine the mineral, vegetable and animal kingdoms, and also the mind of man, and be enabled to gather some practical instruction in these departments of human enquiry". In other words, the elucidation by modern scientific methods of phenomena hitherto regarded as the mysterious acts of a beneficent Creator, was entirely permissible. In his New College lecture, Lankester made crystal clear his belief in evolution, but by repeated acts of the Creator rather than by gradual change. Species of plants and animals are each separately created and are "permanent"; there is no "constant development of new properties in matter and new forms in organic beings". Their permanence is the testimony of the natural world to the direct intervention of the Creator in order to sustain these forms. On the other hand, he explained to the Young

John T. Emmett, Arch'

New College, London.

Fig. 15. New College, Finchley Road, Hampstead.

Men, he was happy to believe that there was an immense span of time between the formation of matter and the appearance of man, because Genesis does not state the time at which God created the Earth, therefore "the geologist has ample verge and scope enough to lay the foundations of the Earth's history". He accepted that in the first period of this history the planets, rocks and seas were formed, and in the second period organisms fitted to marine life were created. In the third period the land appeared and became populated by plants, especially tree-ferns, in prodigious quantities; and because there were few or no animals to produce carbon dioxide, there must have been a greater proportion of the gas in the atmosphere to support the plants. At this time too, "coal beds were deposited for the use of present and future generations" of man. The fourth period saw the creation of reptiles on land, and the fifth, mammals and angiosperms, all these periods spanning aeons of time.

By his statement: "The highest forms of animals are mammalia ... at the head of these mammalia is man", he seems to accept fully that man is fundamentally but an animal, though he is also that final glory, the creature with a soul for whom the whole of the rest of the Creator's works were but a preparation. In his words: " ... it did appear as if the whole of this preparation had been for man's benefit; and I think this conclusion can be fairly arrived at ... It is not too much to suppose that the Creator had thus specially prepared for the existence of man on the surface of the earth". He considered that man's natural needs - food, air and water - were common to the whole animal kingdom and therefore had not been made specifically for him: but substances such as coal and minerals were used exclusively by him for his "artificial" needs, and as they had been deposited millenia before he appeared, they must have been intended specifically for him. Finally, Lankester believed that Christianity was the highest attainment of the human race and "for this Creation was begun". Thus did he manage to weave together into a whole acceptable to himself both as a scientist and as a Christian, the most recent geological discoveries and the idea of "progress" by repeated acts of creation of ever more complex organisms, by an Almighty God whose sole purpose was the welfare of his highest creation, Christian man. His position on the problem of reconciling science and religion was succinctly put:

> Any opposition between the truths of science and scripture ... exists neither in nature nor in revelation, but arises from the imperfection of the individual mind feeling such contradiction. My own conviction is that there is a perfect harmony between the truths of science and those of revelation.

While still attending to his other duties, Lankester had taken on a greater teaching load at the Grosvenor Place School. The record is sketchy[14] but at various times he taught both Botany, with field excursions, and the theory of Anatomy and Physiology, sometimes in addition to, and sometimes instead of, Materia Medica. On two occasions, once in 1846-7 and again in 1848-9, owing to the absence of the usual lecturer, he delivered the greater part of the course on the Practice of Medicine.[15] Medical men were versatile indeed in the mid-nineteenth century. In 1850 he was asked to give the School's Annual Introductory Lecture, which was printed in full, all 10,000 words of it, in the *Medical Times*[16], the lecturer himself also producing it as a pamphlet for private circulation, in which form it earned a very favourable review in the *Athenaeum*.[17]

In a typical gesture, Lankester addressed his lecture specifically to the students, rather than to "the senior members of our profession who have honoured me with their presence". After a preamble on the relationship between physiology and pathology he continued:

> The special function of the medical man ... is to convert the pathological state ... of the human frame into a physiological one, and where this cannot be done, to produce conditions in which life may be prolonged.

In discussing the subjects in which the medical student should be proficient he attacked, indirectly but unambiguously, the precedence given by the élite of the profession (i.e. the Royal College of Physicians) to a classical education. That classical languages and mathematics were "most useful adjuncts to the study of physiology and pathology, I freely admit; but that they are either of them essential to the education of the physician and surgeon, I most emphatically deny"; and that they should be forced upon the profession "as necessary to its practice, I regard as an error calculated deeply to injure its interests." He followed this by a forthright attack on the College's examinations (still without mentioning that institution by name) similar to that quoted by Dr. Crisp.

Next he discussed physics and chemistry as essential basic sciences for the medical man. They were not vital only, he said, in accounting for the way outside forces act on the human body; a knowledge of them has resulted "in the daring enquiry, May not the vital force itself be correlative with physical forces?" His delight, previously hinted at in his early "Essay on the Uncertainty of Medical Science", in the ability of modern science to explain phenomena previously regarded as fundamental mysteries of life, is patent, and was indeed "daring" in an age when religion was still paramount. He went on to give examples of recent discoveries such as photosynthesis (the production of carbohydrates by the action of light on plants); "that electricity, galvanism and magnetism are but manifestations of the same force"; and that chemistry had shown that "many of the phaenomena occurring in the body, which had heretofore been attributed to the action of the vital force, are seen to depend on chemical changes". The boundaries between what had previously been considered discrete phenomena were rapidly being broken down allowing previously undreamed of speculations. Despite these recent advances in science, however, the hand of God could still be seen, and Lankester restated his faith in individual creation and the immutability of species:

It is in the formative force, that power by which each individual species of plant and animal grows into its own form and that of no other, that we have to seek the true source of life and the fountain of all organised experience, but it is precisely here that observations cannot aid us ... and we feel we are in immediate contact with the Deity, and that His hand alone moulds and immediately sustains the varied forms of animal and vegetable life.

There follow long sections on the importance of physiology and pathology, emphasizing that "the normal must be understood before we can conceive of the abnormal", and dilating particularly on three ways in which modern medicine differed from that of the recent past. First, keen and precise observation was essential, and he pressed particularly for the constant use of the microscope.* "What eyes are to the blind", he said, "the microscope is to those who see. Imperfect indeed would be our conception of the anatomy of the human body, if we were dependent on the unassisted eye"; and many of the general theories of disease propounded in the past had been shown by the microscope to be absurd. That Lankester was prepared to give generously of his own time in the cause of microscopy would be apparent in a few years. A second feature of modern medicine was, he said, the use of hearing, made possible by the invention of the stethoscope; and the third, "the application of tests, reagents, and chemical analysis for the purpose of obtaining knowledge of the difference of composition between healthy and diseased structures, and more especially secretions".

After an assault on homoeopathy and its nonsensical and fraudulent principles, for which he had a particular scorn and which he would attack again and again in his writings, he put in a strong plea for the proper planning of trials of new treatments, particularly for the use of large numbers of patients accurately observed. Even so, he was wary of the results of such trials because the accuracy of the results must depend on the reliability of the experimenter, and "the more extraordinary the fact the more necessary it is to investigate the character of the observer". Finally, he assured his young listeners of the nobility of their future profession, exhorted them to work hard and not to succumb to the pleasures of "the smoking-room and gaming-house", to aim high and not to expect wealth;

> Do not imagine that I am addressing you in the language of hyperbole; you will be constantly called upon to exercise your profession where only the spirit of the hero and the martyr can sustain you. The dangers you will have to meet amidst pestilence are greater than those of the soldier in the battlefield, and you will have to meet them alone.

But in the end:

> yours will be the honour to be co-workers with that glorious host of men, by whose toils, and labour, and self-denials, the world has ever been blessed.

Lankester's most important message to his students was to pass on to them his strongly held view, first put forward in his own student days

---

* In this he was ahead of his time, for though a few teaching establishments had used the instrument in lectures and demonstrations since 1840, there was no general recommendation that medical students should be taught microscopy until 1869.[18]

fourteen years earlier in the "Essay on the Uncertainty of Medical Science", that medicine is a science like other sciences, not an art as it had been considered in the past. Physiology and pathology were rapidly removing the necessity for the concept of the Vital Force, and even clinical trials could give reproducible results if planned with proper rigour. His was not the innovative and enquiring mind of the research scientist, but he kept in touch with, and never hesitated to use in his teaching, the methods and discoveries of others, albeit with a proper scepticism on occasion. His long and active interest in the British Association would have have been very important to him in this; and his students must have profited much from a lecturer with so wide a knowledge of recent scientfic advances.

By 1858 Lankester's other commitments had become so heavy that he must have found his total work load excessive, for he resigned from the School, which itself finally closed its doors five years later. By then St. George's and St. Mary's Hospitals had their own medical schools, University College and King's College Hospitals were well established, and the need for private medical schools had passed.

At the British Association in the late 1840s, Lankester had read papers on a variety of subjects including one of his recurring interests, plants of possible economic importance to man. In 1851, when the Association met at Ipswich[19] (a town which he must have visited in his childhood, for it is only a few miles from Woodbridge), he reverted to one of his favourite topics, the structure of wood and the movement of sap. Expressing the same sceptism about a "vital force" to this wider audience as he had to his own students he said:

> It is unphilosophical to speak of vitality as a force when it could not be demonstrated to exist, and especially when physical forces are capable of explaining the phaenomenon.

It is interesting that at this meeting what must be one of the earliest public warnings of the danger of deforestation in the tropics is given. A committee set up by the Association to investigate the problem reported back:

> 1. That over large portions of the Indian Empire, there is at present an almost uncontrolled destruction of the indigenous forests in progress due to the careless habits of the native population.
> 2. That ... where supervision is excercised, considerable improvement has already taken place.
> 3. That these improvements may be extended by ... the planting of seedlings in the place of mature trees removed ... prohibition of cutting down until the trees are well grown.

4. That in a country to which maintenance of its water supplies is of such extreme importance, the indiscriminate clearance of trees around the localities whence those supplies are derived is greatly to be deprecated.

Lankester must have taken the opportunity of the Ipswich meeting to give his young family a seaside holiday on the bracing coast of his home county, for his son Ray, four years old at the time, always remembered being carried over the rocky Felixstowe beach at low tide by his father's friend, Thomas Henry Huxley.[20] In later years Huxley was to do much to start Ray on his distinguished scientific career.

Lankester's scientific standing was now increasingly being recognised. In 1851 he was serving a two-year spell on the Council of the Linnean Society (though its brief minutes do not record any contribution from him); he was awarded the Honorary Degree of Ll.D by Amherst College, Massachusetts,[21] probably through the good offices of its President, Edward Hitchcock, who Lankester had met during the former's tour of England the previous year;[22] and he was invited to take part in the summer lectures of the Royal Botanic Society of London[23].

This Society, now almost forgotten, had been founded in 1838 to take over and develop into a botanic garden the Inner Circle at Regent's Park, which up to then had been used as a nursery. By the 1850s the new gardens had been laid out and had become popular pleasure grounds with annual shows, but the Society had introduced no wider interests such as promoting the collection of plants, or providing gardeners with an advisory service.[24] For a few years it did attempt some teaching, though whether its lectures were intended for members only or for the general public is not stated in the very incomplete minutes which survive.[25] The first existing mention of the Lecture Committee is in 1853, when it recommended that in the following year a course of not more than eight lectures be given on Fridays in May and June, and that "Dr. Lankester and Mr. Bentley be requested to undertake the office of Lecturers" at five guineas per lecture. The Lecture Committee does not seem to have existed before 1850 or after 1853, therefore the likelihood is that Lankester lectured from 1851 to 1854. As to the Society, it survived until 1928, when the government refused to extend its lease on the Garden. Having no other raison d'être, it finally sold its assets and closed in 1931.

The Westminster Medical Society, of which Lankester had been Vice-President in 1850, was taken over that year by the much older Medical Society of London, and 1851 found him on the Council of the new body, which held its meetings, like the Westminster, on winter Saturdays, but at 32a, George Street, Hanover Square. According to reports in the medical press he took as active a part in the affairs of this Society as he had in the Westminster, acting as Vice-President in 1852-1853 and sitting on the

QUARTERLY   JOURNAL

OF

MICROSCOPICAL   SCIENCE:

EDITED BY

EDWIN   LANKESTER,   M.D.,   F.R.S.,   &c.,

AND

E. RAY LANKESTER, B.A. Oxon., F.R.M.S.

VOLUME X.—New Series.

With Illustrations on Wood and Stone.

LONDON
JOHN CHURCHILL AND SONS, NEW BURLINGTON STREET
1870.

Fig. 16. Title page of the 1870 volume of the *Quarterly Journal of Microscopical Science*, edited by Edwin and Ray Lankester.

Council for four of the next seven years; only from 1862 did he cease to hold office. He was often in the chair at meetings and exhibited apparatus and photographs. Each year the Society appointed four of its members as "Lecturers", and Lankester held this office in 1856 and 1857.

Not content with his numerous existing voluntary responsibilities, he now undertook yet another. The Microscopical Society of London, to become the Royal Microscopical Society in 1866, was founded in 1839. The date at which Lankester joined is unknown, but as his studies on the structure of wood show, he must have been using a microscope since at least 1842 and, when his penchant for joining societies is taken into account, it is difficult to believe that he held aloof from this one for long. We know that he retired from its Council in 1855, so it is likely that he was already on it in 1853 when he and Dr. George Busk, a noted protozoologist who had been President in 1848, offered to start a new journal to be called the *Quarterly Journal of Microscopical Science*, which could include the Society's *Transactions* and be supplied free to members in return for a contribution from the Society for expenses.[26] The offer was accepted and the arrangement continued until 1868, when the Society broke away to publish its own *Journal*. Busk took this opportunity to resign and Ray Lankester, then aged 21, took his place (Fig. 16). Three years later the father and son partnership broke up, Edwin retiring having been editor for 18 years, and Ray taking over full responsibility.

Edwin's exertions on behalf of the British Association, the Medical Society of London and the Microscopical Society were, like his duties as a vestryman, time-consuming, and he undoubtedly enjoyed them, but they did not add to his income. It was probably as much to ease his financial position as to keep his hand in as a physician that, in 1853, he accepted the post of Physician to the English Widows' Fund Assurance Office, one of numerous assurance companies which were springing up at the time, and held it for at least five years. The Fund's offices were in Fleet Street and its prestigious patron was H.R.H. the Duke of Cambridge. The *Medical Directory* for 1855 contains a fulsome, unsigned article on life assurance, asking doctors to recommend it to their patients, pointing out the dependence of each profession on the other, and ending:

> So much do we consider the furtherance of the principle of Life Assurance to be in the hands of the Medical Profession and the Clergy, that we hold it to be the duty of the one never to retire from a convalescent patient without drawing attention to the advantage of Life Assurance.

The article is followed by advertisements for a number of assurance companies, including the English Widows', which appeared for the last time in 1858, still naming Lankester as its Physician.

Chapter Six

Cholera   1849-1856

Cholera had been a scourge in India since the turn of the ninteenth century, had spread like wildfire through the countries of the Far East thereafter, and had reached Europe by 1830. In Britain the first outbreak appeared in some of our major cities in 1832. Late in 1847 a second wave of the disease reached Russia, and the alarm bells began to ring in this country. The following year the disease struck, again attacking most of our cities. In London, despite warnings, the Board of Health had just two medical inspectors to cover the whole metropolis, and the local Boards of Guardians would do nothing, in spite of government urging, because legally they could not be compelled to act. It was not until the Board of Health finally issued specific orders to vestries that local action was taken. Edwin Chadwick, Commissioner of the Metropolitan Commission of Sewers, who was already waging an energetic war against the disgusting state of London's blocked and broken sewers, ordered that they be flushed into the Thames more energetically than ever, giving no thought to the fact that the river was the sole water supply for tens of thousands of citizens.[1] So cholera raged through the foetid slums creating terror among their helpless inhabitants and fear even among the higher classes, a few of whom were also struck down. Both its cause and its means of spread were unknown, conflicting theories abounded, and inevitably there was no agreement on methods of control.

At that date the theory of spontaneous generation was only just being laid to rest, bacteria had not yet been discovered, and the only malady known to be caused by a living organism was the muscardine disease of silkworms, which the Italian, Agostina Bassi, had shown experimentally in 1838 to be the result of infection by a fungus, *Botrytis paradoxa*, (later *B. bassiana*).[2,3] Pasteur's classic "Memoire sur les Corpuscules organisées qui existent dans l'Atmosphère" did not appear until 1860, or Robert Koch's epoch-making "Aetiology of traumatic infective Disease" until 1878, and even then most people found his ideas difficult to accept. Koch did not discover the actual cause of cholera, the bacterium *Vibrio cholerae*, until 1884.

It was of course, recognized that diseases of all sorts, including fevers, were far more common among the poor than among the better off, and that morbidity and mortality rates were far higher in the seething slums that in the less crowded and more salubrious parts of cities, yet it took many years and much dispute to connect this phenomenon with the filth and overcrowding of the impoverished areas. The stumbling block appears to have been the belief in the theory of contagion as the sole means by which the infective diseases could be passed on; that is, that a material substance, or "poison", must be passed from a diseased to a healthy person by direct contact. Examples of such diseases were smallpox and syphilis, and the obvious way to control them was by quarantine, a procedure which the authorities considered should be applied to cholera too. Soon a strong anti-contagionist school arose whose adherents classified cholera with "fever", yellow fever and plague as "epidemic", that is, occurring in certain localities and seasons and associated with environmental factors, especially the state of the atmosphere. Anti-contagionists believed firmly that filth was the primary cause of disease, and that the stench and "miasmata" to which it gave rise were the source of the poisons which caused the diseases. Where these poisons were dispersed in well ventilated rooms, wide streets and open spaces they caused little damage; only in the overcrowded and filthy slums did problems arise. The anti-contagionists campaigned vigorously for sanitary legislation and a drastic clean-up of the cities.[4]

Tremendous arguments went on between the protagonists of the two theories, with the anti-contagionists eventually winning. On the whole, the medical profession at the time was interested only in finding cures for the infectious diseases; it was the sanitarians such as William Farr, the Compiler of Abstracts (or statistician) working for the General Register Office, Edwin Chadwick, the civil servant whose name is inextricably bound up with the government's attempts at sanitary reform, and Southwood Smith, the predecessor of all medical officers of health, who believed in prevention rather than cure and were passionate advocates of the sanitary cause. Farr (1807-1883) had trained as a doctor, finishing his studies in Paris, where hygiene and medical statistics were part of the curriculum, so he was well qualified for the part he would play in the sanitary movement. It was he who, in 1842, first coined the term "zymotic" to cover all infectious diseases, whether contagious or epidemic, a term which was taken into common use all through the middle years of the nineteenth century. He regarded infectious disease as a form of fermentation or "zymosis" in which poisons of unknown composition, which could perpetuate themselves, were propagated either by inhalation or by contact and were generated by putrifying organic matter. Farr was an anti-contagionist who gave a unifying structure to the theory. In an age of rapid scientific advance the zymotic theory proved highly adaptable, for as knowledge grew it was easy to replace the "poisons" of the theory, first with "particles" and then with "self-propagating particles", until such time as bacteria proper were discovered.[4]

Against this background it is remarkable that as early as 1849 both Dr. John Snow of London and Dr. William Budd of Bristol published independently of one another papers announcing that the cause of cholera was a living organism of a distinct species, capable of reproducing itself in the human intestine, and disseminated through infected drinking water.[5] It would be some years before Snow could vindicate this brilliant piece of deduction and many more before it was universally accepted.

John Snow (Fig. 17) was born in 1813. At the tender age of 14 he was apprenticed to a surgeon in Newcastle, and had completed four years of his indenture when the 1831-1832 cholera epidemic struck the city. His master sent him to take charge of the outbreak at Killingworth Colliery and it was there, between his ministrations to the colliers, that he made many of the observations which were to stand him in such good stead in London later. After several moves he eventually arrived in London in 1838, qualified M.R.C.S., L.S.A. from Westminster Hospital, and joined the Westminster Medical Society where, over the years, he read a number of excellent and original papers. It must have been there, too, that he and Lankester first met. He obtained his higher medical qualifications at University College and went into practice both privately and at Charing Cross Hospital and then, in 1846, news arrived from America of the successful use of ether for painless surgery. The idea appealed immensely to Snow, who immediately began his pioneering work on anaesthesia.* Then came the 1848 cholera outbreak, Snow's attention was diverted to the disease, and the following year he wrote his epoch-making tract, *On the mode of Communication of Cholera.*[7,8]

William Budd (Fig. 18), a Devon man by birth, was a few years older than Lankester and Snow, and obtained his M.D. at Edinburgh in 1838. By the time he settled in Bristol in 1841 he had had a wide experience in several branches of medicine in both England and France. In Bristol, Budd was Physician to St. Peter's Hospital and the Bristol Royal Infirmary, and Lecturer in Medicine at the Bristol Medical College. He carried out pioneering studies on the distinction between typhus and typhoid, but is probably best known for his work on the infectivity of the latter. In 1849, when cholera broke out in Bristol, the Health of Towns Commission reported that the city was "the third most unhealthy town in England", and that "viewed as a sanitary question, there are few if any large towns ...

---

* It was he who, in 1853 and 1857, administered chloroform to Queen Victoria for the births of Prince Leopold and Princess Beatrice.

Fig. 17. Dr. John Snow.

Fig. 18. Dr. William Budd.

Fig. 19. Portrait of Dr Lankester which appeared in the *Illustrated London News* on his appointment as Coroner.

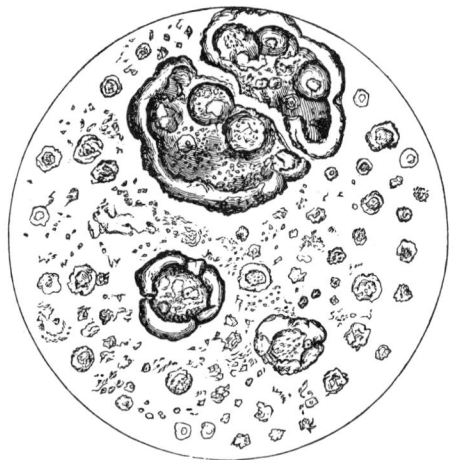

Fig. 20. William Budd's drawing of the "cholera fungus" in various stages of development.

in which the supply of water was so inadequate". Budd threw himself wholeheartedly into the fight against the disease, urging the destruction or disinfection of the excreta of the sick and of contaminated bedding, clothing and other fomites, and the provision of a pure water supply.[9]

Of the many theories then in vogue as to the cause of cholera, only Snow and Budd had stated categorically that it was due to a living organism, but neither of them had made any suggestion as to the nature of that organism. Any identification of it would depend on the comparatively new science, to medicine at least, of microscopy, and while the microscopes then available were of remarkably high quality, their usefulness was limited by the so far poorly developed fixing and staining methods, which would show little improvement until after 1860.[10] This must be borne in mind when considering the fungoid theory of cholera. The theory originated in Bristol, where the Microscopical Sub-Committee of the Bristol Medical and Chirological Society was in the habit of meeting at the houses of its members, there to submit to microscopic examination and subsequent discussion any object of current medical interest. On 9 July, 1849, the Sub-Committee was meeting at William Budd's home, and its attention was focused on the evacuations and vomit from cholera patients. Two members found in them identical bodies which they had never seen before, and their findings were published by Dr. Brittan a few months later. Meanwhile Budd had discovered the same bodies in contaminated water but not in pure, and Dr. J. G. Swayne had found them in air. According to Brittan, John Quekett, a greatly respected member of the Microscopical Society of London, was the first person to state that the bodies were "fungoid". The cholera fungus theory then began in earnest at the Bristol Literary and Philosophical Institute, of which Budd and Swayne were founding members, and which had close associations with London.[10] In particular Budd knew (through his brother George) the President of the Microscopical Society of London, George Busk, and other medical members of the Bristol Institute were often in London. Busk was already a friend of Lankester's[11] (though it would be some years before the two of them became joint editors of the *Quarterly Journal of Microscopical Science*), thus Lankester was early involved in the controversy. And a lively controversy it was, both the medical and lay presses being inundated with letters, occasionally of considerable virulence.

Budd, as might be expected after his prediction that cholera was caused by a living organism, was whole-heartedly in support of the fungoid theory, despite some contradictory findings; and Swayne published a careful study of the bodies. He considered that the three sizes of body which he found were cells of different ages, and that they were produced from a mulberry-shaped parent cell, the "perfect cholera cell", of which he sent samples to Lankester and Busk (Fig. 20). Now it must have been very tempting, before the discovery of bacteria, to attribute cholera or any other "zymotic" disease to infection by pathogenic fungi, for not only were they large enough to be easily visible by the microscopical techniques of the time, but the only infectious diseases whose origins were known were caused by fungi. The muscardine disease of silkworms has already been mentioned; in addition to this, French and German workers showed a few years later that ringworm and favus were also caused by fungi. On the other hand it is probable that few medical men had much experience of the microscopical appearance of these organisms and so could easily confuse them with artifacts. So a number of doctors, including Swayne and Budd, became ardent proponents of the fungoid theory of cholera.

Lankester, as we have seen, had taken more than a passing interest in fungi in his capacity as a naturalist. In fact, an article "On progress in organic chemistry" written in 1849,[12] shows that he certainly regarded the fungal origin of some plant diseases as proven and would have liked to find similar causes of animal disease. So he was doubtless well aware of the appearance of these organisms under the microscope, and when he examined Swayne's "fungal bodies" he had no hesitation in pronouncing them to be altered human epithelial cells.[13] Busk, on the other hand, identified them as starch grains and pieces of wheat husk such as he could demonstrate in a loaf bought in the market; Swayne's "perfect cholera cells" he thought were uredos, the spores of the rust fungus which causes a disease of wheat. Lankester, while not entirely abandoning his own opinion, put forward and endorsed Busk's at a meeting of the Westminster Medical Society a few days later,[11] adding that:

> ... he felt convinced of the correctness of Mr. Busk's inference, that no new organism had yet been demonstrated to exist in the body of those affected with cholera. All the bodies that had been observed by the microscope were evidently introduced by the food or were natural products of the mucous membrane.

During the cholera fungus crisis the members of the Westminster Society, on the Committee of which Lankester was sitting at the time, and in which Snow was very active, were working overtime, for not only was it holding its normal weekly meetings, but frequent emergency meetings as well. Despite opposition, Swayne still held firmly to his theory, and in an attempt to refute Busk's identification of his "perfect cholera cells" as uredos, he sent some material to the Rev. M. J. Berkeley, the father of British mycology, who had shown in 1846 that the potato murrain which had caused the Irish famine was the work of a pathogenic fungus. Berkeley duly confirmed that the cells were not uredos but could not say what they were; they were certainly not fungi.[14]

At the height of the excitement over the fungoid theory the *Lancet* printed a furious letter from "A member of the Bristol Microscopical Society" defending Drs. Budd, Swayne and Brittan and their careful observations, and attacking Busk for disposing of "the so-called cholera fungus in a very off-hand manner" and for insinuating that his deprived provincial brethren lacked the advantage of the more sophisticated instruments available in the metropolis.[15] But it was not long afterwards that the fungoid theory faded from the pages of the medical journals. Lankester continued to make occasional references to it in lectures on broader subjects, while Snow never seems to have taken a great interest in the controversy; he was an epidemiologist, not a microscopist.

Despite the 1848-1849 cholera outbreak and Edwin Chadwick's frantic attempts to bring in sanitary legislation for London, vested interests had seen to it that little was achieved. London's water was supplied by eight joint stock companies whose services were disgraceful. Only the wealthier districts were adequately supplied; the homes of the poor either had no piped water at all and relied on wells which were thick with scum and sewage, or had one stand-pipe to every 20 or 30 houses supplying water for one hour a day, often for as little as three days a week (Fig. 21). Some of these stand-pipes were supplied from the rivers Chadwell and Lee, and although they contained the pollution from 20 miles of villages along their banks, the water was the best in London. Others were supplied from the Thames itself, with its burden of filth from the 209 public sewers which discharged into it, the slaughter-house refuse, and the industrial waste from every sort of factory from tanneries to chemical works.[16]

In 1850 the pioneering microscopist, Dr. Arthur Hassell, published an illustrated booklet entitled *A Microscopical Examination of the Water Supplied to the Inhabitants of London and the Surrounding Districts*, which showed for the first time the mass of organic refuse and living animalcules in the drinking water of the metropolis (Fig. 22). The booklet attracted a great deal of attention, and Chadwick invited Hassell to give evidence before the Parliamentary Committee then enquiring into the state of London's water.[17] At last, in 1852, the Metropolitan Water Act was passed. It was a weak Act, but at least it did require that the water companies should cease to draw water from the Thames below Teddington Lock by 1856, and with that threat hanging over them the companies had to act. To this end the directors of the London (Watford) Spring Water Company hired the services of Dr. Lankester and Dr. Redfern to investigate their water source and submit reports. Lankester, already an experienced microscopist, followed Hassell's lead and reported "On the results of the microscopical examinations of the organic matters and solid contents of waters supplied from the Thames and other sources."[18] The report was published in 1852, with the comment that this was the first occasion on which such an

Fig. 21. Queueing for water at a standpipe in East London. The parishioners of St. James's, Westminster, suffered under the same conditions.

Fig. 22. The microscopical appearance of Thames water as it appeared to a contemporary cartoonist.

Fig. 23. The deposit from a sample of drinking water seen under the microscope. From *On Food*.

extensive microscopic examination had been made public by a supplier, chemical examination having previously been thought sufficient.

As well as water from the Watford springs, Lankester examined water from five other sources. His method was to collect half a gallon of water in a stoppered bottle and allow it to settle for 12 to 24 hours in a cool place, when living creatures visible to the naked eye were pipetted off. If there was a large deposit he pipetted that off directly; if only a small one, he syphoned off the supernatant first. The deposit was then mounted on a slide and examined under the low and high powers of the microscope (Fig. 23). All the five London supplies were badly contaminated, even those from above Teddington Lock. "The surface drainage of the most richly manured country in the world", he wrote, "and the sewers and drains of a hundred villages and towns, are emptied into the Thames" above the lock. And he listed all the microscopic plants and animals he found. The Watford water, however, was clean and eminently suitable for a public supply. Soon after their study, Lankester and Redfern used their experience to publish an article in the *Lancet*[19] on "The microscope as a test of the purity of drinking water."

The 1852 Water Act proved to be too little and too late. That year cholera broke out again in Poland and in America, and here the Board of Health sounded the alert, the medical profession dropped its emphasis on cure and worked with the authorities on prevention, and for once the vestries were co-operative.[20] In September, 1853, the disease began its onslaught at Newcastle and Gateshead, by 1854 it was ravaging the South London slums, and John Snow was in the thick of the investigations there. Then, on 1 September, with no forewarning, the inhabitants of the Golden Square-Berwick Street district of Westminster (Fig. 14) (where Lankester had lived when he started work in London), in the parish of St. James's, were subjected to what must have been the most terrible and concentrated outbreak of cholera this country ever saw. More than 105 people living and working in an area of a few hundred square yards died in ten days; by the middle of the month the outbreak was over. (Fig. 24).

Fig. 24. Death certificate of Susannah Eley, one time resident of Broad Street, who died of cholera having had water from the pump delivered to her daily in her new abode.

Fig. 25. The Broad Street pump.

Fig. 26. Cholera in Broad Street.

On 7 September John Snow, whose home was at 18 Sackville Street (Fig. 14), not ten minutes walk from Berwick Street, and who was a parishioner of St. James's, rushed to the site of the disaster, surveyed the local circumstances, and concluded that a very popular pump in Broad Street (now Broadwick Street), known for its constant supply of clear, bright water, was the source of the infection (Figs 25, 26). That evening he obtained an audience of the Board of Guardians and put his case so eloquently that despite the fact that it was in direct contradiction to the general conviction that cholera was the result of the miasmata arising from filth accumulated in confined spaces, the Board ordered the removal of the pump handle the next day, 8 September. In fact, the mortality figures show that the outbreak, following its normal course, had already passed its peak by then, and the removal of the pump handle saved few if any lives. But the detailed epidemiological investigations which followed this famous episode of "John Snow and the Broad Street pump" established once and for all that cholera is a water-borne disease, even though it was many years before the fact was universally accepted.

It is less well known that without the intervention of Edwin Lankester in his capacity as vestryman, and of the local curate, Henry Whitehead, Snow would have been unable to obtain the proof of his brilliant deduction. At a Vestry meeting held on 2 November, after the outbreak was over, Lankester gave notice of the following motion:

> That a Committe of this Vestry be appointed for the purpose of investigating the causes, arising out of the present sanitary conditions of the parish, of the late outbreak of cholera in the districts of Golden Square and Berwick Street.

At the next meeting three weeks later, after a vigorous discussion, the motion was agreed to, and the Cholera Inquiry Committee, consisting of six vestrymen and the two churchwardens under Lankester's chairmanship, was set up. Altogether it held 14 meetings between 25 November, 1854, and 25 July 1855, and its final report, with separate sections by Snow and Whitehead, is a model of clarity and ·conciseness. However, the Committee only just survived to produce a report, or even to hold its second meeting, for on 14 December the Board of Guardians true to its reputation, wrote to the Vestry regretting the setting up of the Committee, first on financial grounds - the Poor Rate, said the Guardians, was wholly unable to meet the expense; and secondly they objected:

> ... in greater degree on account of the mischievous effects which a renewed investigation of the subject so recently made by the Government officers is calculated to inflict on the Householders and Inhabitants of the locality,

now but slowly recovering from the serious depression of their trade and employment and by whom the inquiry instituted by the Vestry is consequently viewed with feelings of dissatisfaction and alarm.*

In other words, the tradesmen and better off householders realized that they were to blame for the state of filth and disrepair they had allowed their parish to fall into, and did not wish attention drawn to themselves. A motion that the Committee should discontinue its work was immediately put forward in the Vestry, for this would save a great deal of money, and it was only after considerable discussion, with Lankester doubtless fighting hard for his Committee's life, that the motion was defeated.[21,22] Without the Committee, Snow's epidemiological studies would have ended with the end of the outbreak, for he had no official standing in the parish and would have been in no position to make the necessary enquiries.

The Committee began its work by considering all existing documentary evidence, including an analysis of the well-waters of the parish which had been carried out by Lankester in October, very soon after the outbreak was over. It is not clear whether it was Snow or the Vestry who had requested the analysis, but Lankester had shown that of the several wells in the affected district, only that feeding the Broad Street pump had contained organic matter. This sample became cloudy on standing for a short time, and Lankester showed that the cloudiness was caused by the profuse growth of a filamentous fungus[23] (Chapter 8). He did not claim that the fungus was the cause of the cholera outbreak, but that it indicated that the water was sufficiently impure to be injurious to health. The Committee also tried to obtain the information on the outbreak collected at the time by the Government inspectors and mentioned by the Board of Guardians in their letter of protest to the Vestry, but this was refused point blank. Lesser men might have given up at this point, but Lankester and the Committee decided to press ahead using any information which was available. Again we can see Lankester's determination propelling them onwards, for though there is no record that it was he who overcame each and every obstacle, such would be entirely consistent with his character. We have seen how he obtained his education by his own dogged determination and how, when beaten in the unequal struggle with the Royal College of Physicians, he set about using his talents to find other means of earning a living. His future career would show up these qualities even more strongly.

---

* Sometime after I had worked out for myself, from the original documents, Lankester's part in this episode, I came across the papers of S.W.P. Chave[22] who, using the same sources, had come to similar conclusions, but with special reference to Whitehead.

The Committee's first attempt to obtain the information it needed was by means of a questionnaire sent to each householder, asking him about the family's living conditions and the number of deaths suffered. Predictably, this approach failed dismally to attain its purpose, and the Committee then decided that only a house-to-house visitation could elicit the necessary facts, to which end eight new members were co-opted including Snow and the Rev. Whitehead. Snow was, of course, already well known to Lankester through the Westminster Medical Society, and doubtless, too, because they were now near neighbours, Lankester having moved to 8, Savile Row that year.

It was Whitehead who would prove to be the most indispensible member of the Committee. He was 29 at the time, and was Curate of St. Luke's, Berwick Street, within the parish of St. James's (Fig. 27). St. Luke's was a new church, having been built only in 1838 to serve what was then the most densely populated district in London.* In the previous century the district had been developed with large houses for the better off (Fig. 28), but by the 1850s, though its external appearance had not altered, it had undergone a serious social decline, the houses had been divided and subdivided into tenements and workshops, and there was gross overcrowding. Whitehead was an exemplary curate who knew all his parishioners and had already published his own report of the cholera disaster within a few weeks of the end of the outbreak, including street by street mortality figures he had collected himself. He greeted Snow's theory with total disbelief, and once on the Committee he set out to disprove it in his own meticulous way. Suffice it to say that it was the results Whitehead obtained from his house-to-house visits and his careful tracing of those who had moved away, supplemented by the findings of Snow himself and of the Committee, which finally gave Snow the proof he needed that the Broad Street pump was the source of the outbreak. One mystery which the main enquiry had not solved was how the pump had become polluted in the first place, and again it was Whitehead's dogged persistence which provided the answer. The pump was adjacent to No. 40, Broad Street (Fig. 29), and Whitehead ascertained that just before the outbreak started a baby living there had died of diarrhoea. Its mother had been in the habit of tipping the water in which she washed its nappies into the cesspool in front of the house. On investigation it was discovered that this cesspool was only three feet from the well which fed the pump, and that the pool's contents were seeping into the well through the decaying brickwork. Whitehead's own results eventually convinced him that Snow was right

---

* The church was demolished in 1936, a life span of just 98 years.

Fig. 27. St. Luke's Church, Berwick Street.

Fig. 28. Nos 45 to 39, Broad Street, in 1878.

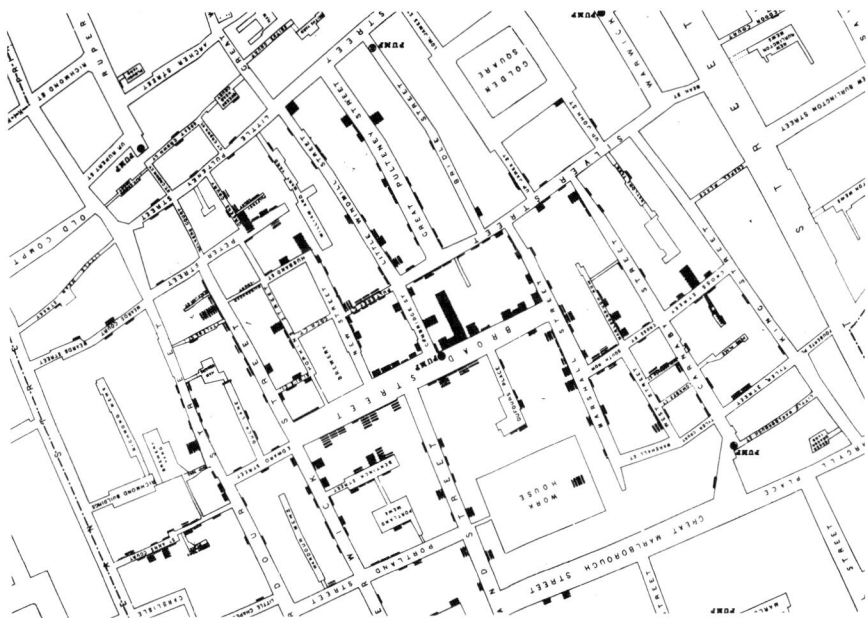

Fig. 29. Part of John Snow's map of the Broad Street district with the fatal pump at the centre. The black columns represent the number of cholera victims in those houses.

and he offered the latter a handsome apology. Lankester, though fully accepting Snow's theory, continued to believe that drinking water was only one of the ways in which cholera was disseminated

At the Vestry Meeting on 9 August, 1855, Lankester presented the Cholera Committee's 175-page Report,[24] speaking to it at some length and quoting parts. Among its recommendations was that "a medical inspector of the parish be appointed", a suggestion which was to be fulfilled with perhaps unexpected speed. Such was the public spiritedness of the Vestry that the Report was accepted only by the casting vote of the chairman, and only by so narrow a margin did this important document ever see the light of day. Snow had indeed much for which to thank Lankester. Despite a protest from the Board of Guardians, the sum of £20 was voted for the publication of 500 copies of the Report, but at the next meeting of the Vestry the Committee's Secretary announced that this was totally inadequate, and after a long debate the sum of £70 was granted, with the hope that some of the costs would be defrayed by sales to the public, a vain hope, for in April, 1856, the Vestry requested £170 12s 7d from the

Poor Rate to cover the whole cost of the enquiry.[21,22] The newly founded *Journal of Public Health* was much impressed by the Report.

The year 1855 saw the passing of the Metropolis Local Management Act, which, in the matter of London's health, brought up to date the Public Health Act of 1848. Under that Act, Liverpool and London had each appointed a Medical Officer of Health, the first two in Britain; the new Act not only empowered, but compelled, every vestry in London to do the same. The officers' duties would be to inspect and report periodically on the sanitary condition of the parishes and "to ascertain the existence of diseases, more especially epidemics ...". To carry out these duties fully the medical officer would be expected to inform the public of conditions in the parish by the publication of annual reports, to carry out house-to-house visits in epidemic areas, to take charge of vaccination campaigns,* to inspect schools, factories and workshops, to superintend the removal of cesspools, the improvement of sewers etc., and to regulate slaughterhouses, food adulteration and other nuisances.[26]

As well as attending to health matters, the Act also regulated the constitution of vestries, requiring that each ward in the parish should be represented. At its first meeting under the Act, on 29 November, 1855, the membership of the new Vestry of St. James was read out, with Lankester sitting for Church Ward. On 3 January, 1856, the Vestry continued a previous discussion on the requirement that they should appoint a medical officer of health, a matter which clearly did not meet with their whole-hearted support. A salary of £100 per annum was suggested (the post would be part time) and, though they realized the sum would probably be inadequate, they decided to keep to it until the duties of the officer were clearer. An advertisement was placed in *The Times* and three applications were received, all from doctors resident in the parish, one of whom was Lankester. A week later Lankester and one of the other applicants were interviewed and Lankester was appointed by 25 votes to 7. The appointment reflects some credit on the Vestry and much on Lankester's personality, for the vestrymen knew him well by now and must have realized that, charming though he was, nothing would deter him from seeking out the evils in his district and insisting that neither inertia nor financial considerations should be barriers to their rectification. As a servant of the Vestry, he now resigned his seat as vestryman and wrote to his erstwhile colleagues thanking them for his appointment.

At last, at the age of 42, he had found a job which would satisfy his philanthropic ideals and allow him to use to the full his medical, scientific and social skills. He would spend the rest of his life making every effort to improve the lot of the poor and downtrodden in a parish in which

---

* Vaccination against smallpox became compulsory in 1853.

extremes of wealth and poverty existed cheek by jowl. What is more, as the first incumbent of the post, he could shape it according to his own ideas of the priorities before him, his success being limited only by his power to coax or bludgeon money from a reluctant Vestry.

Towards the end of his time as a vestryman, when he was also teaching at New College and the Grosvenor Place School and working for the British Association and the Microscopical Society, as well as playing a leading part in the investigations of the cholera outbreak, Lankester had also become an influential medical politician and had continued his scientific writings. These two facets of his career must be chronicled before his tenure of the post of Medical Officer of Health is considered.

Chapter Seven

Medical Politician   1853-1858

The twenty or thirty years prior to the passing of the Medical Reform Act in 1858 were times of tremendous upheaval and reappraisal in the medical profession, as it tried to shake off its mediaeval structure and come to terms with the needs of a rapidly industrializing country and an increasingly science based medicine. Lankester was in the thick of the turmoil and, for the final six years at least, played a very active part in the politicking which inevitably went on. Before the Act was passed there were 21 different licensing bodies for doctors with widely varying requirements for registration; none of the licenses granted by these bodies had legal backing or qualified the holder to practise in all parts of the country. Equally, there was no universally recognized system of education, so that members of the public had no guarantee that their practitioner was properly qualified, and doctors who were fully qualified, and even very experienced practitioners in one part of the country, had to sit some trivial examination (as Lankester had had to do) if they wished to practise in another part. Physicians were not required to know anything of surgery or, perhaps worse, surgeons of medicine. The fundamental need of the profession was, therefore, for qualificiations of a uniformly high standard which would be recognized throughout the United Kingdom, and a nation-wide register on which all qualified men would be entered regardless of their speciality: once having attained this register, a doctor would be entitled to practise anywhere in the country. Clearly such a reform would gravely undermine the ancient privileges of the Royal Colleges (or corporations, as they were known), and they were prepared to fight for their traditional rights. However, the general practitioners, now the most numerous body of medical men in the country, together with the provincial specialists, were increasingly resentful of the Colleges, seeing them as a minority dictatorship ruling the majority of the profession without its consent.

As early as the 1830s medical reform societies had been founded all over the country, and in London the British Medical Association (not the present body, and confined to London despite its name) was trying to co-ordinate the work of all the others, and was organising petitions to

Parliament and delegations to ministers. In 1841 it had convened a conference of all the reform associations, including the Provincial Medical and Surgical Association (PMSA). This organisation had been founded in 1832, with the backing of the Society of Apothecaries, to cater for the provincial doctors who were ignored by the Colleges. The PMSA, led by Sir Charles Hastings, an eminent physician from Worcester, had been founded as a friendly and scientific society and was not at first interested in medical reform; but by the 1841 conference its attitude had changed, though it was still not as radical as the London BMA. In fact, while the London BMA aimed to destroy the Colleges by removing their power to license practitioners, the PMSA wished only to democratize them and regulate their examination systems. In the mid-1840s the London BMA joined up with another association and gradually faded from the scene, and by 1851, both the Royal Colleges and Dr. Wakely, the battling founder and editor of the *Lancet*, had acknowledged that, within the profession, the PMSA was the leading body working for medical reform.[1]

In keeping with its name, the PMSA had branches all over the country with the exception of London, though a few London doctors joined as individual members. But there were many general practitioners and others in London who felt as strongly about the need to contain the overweening powers of the corporations as did their provincial brethren, and with the disappearance of the London BMA they had no means of making their views known. This was the principle reason for the setting up, in January, 1853, of the Metropolitan Counties Branch of the PMSA. In addition, a foothold in London would be convenient for the Association, for it had recently decided to transfer the publication of its journal, the *Provincial Medical and Surgical Journal*, from Worcester to London and to change its name to *Association Medical Journal (AMJ)*. As there were already a number of medical societies in London, it was considered unnecessary for the new Branch to include the reading of papers among its activities, leaving it plenty of time to devote to other matters. It did not waste its opportunities. No sooner was it founded than it began to make its presence felt, not only on medical reform on which it set up its own committee, but on the internal re-organization of its own parent body. From records of its meetings in the *AMJ*, the *Lancet*, and the *Medical Times and Gazette* (*MTG*) it is possible to piece together a remarkably detailed account of the machinations of this Branch and of its individual members.

The first time Lankester's name appears is as chairman of the Branch's Medical Reform Committee in June, 1853,[2] but from the dominant role he was playing then, it seems that he must have been a founder member of the Branch. By its second Annual Meeting on 25 July, 1854, (marked by a dinner at which Lankester proposed one of the toasts) it is clear that the Branch had already dissected and rewritten the rules of its parent body with great thoroughness, for it appointed a deputation of three, including Lankester, to attend the Association's Annual Meeting at Manchester in September and discuss its suggested changes with the General Council. One of these changes would give the Branch considerable autonomy by allowing it, rather than the Council of the Association, to decide whether or not to admit a candidate to membership; another was nothing less than a proposal to change the name of the Association from "Provincial" to "British", so that it could legitimately include, not only London, but Scotland and Ireland.

At the Manchester Meeting the PMSA's founder, Sir Charles Hastings, and the older members strongly opposed this suggestion, while the younger members supported it. The Metropolitan Counties Branch was castigated as the meddling upstart it undoubtedly was, and when Lankester rose to second the motion, it was to pour oil on troubled waters. He would have preferred, he said, not to undertake this duty, on the grounds that he was a member of a Branch which was regarded "with the kind of suspicion with which revolutionary propagandists are sometimes looked on". After explaining the benefits of the proposed change in a calm and reasoned manner he continued:

> We want to bind each other together in a common bond of union. We have moral objects in view; we have also political objects in view; we want to have our profession put in proper relation to the state; and this never will be achieved until a great Association like this embraces all the members of the profession. It is upon this ground we should be more desirous of appropriating to ourselves the name "British".[3]

He ended his conciliatory speech by suggesting that if the proposal was likely to split the Association the change should be postponed until the founders "are gone, and have left nothing but their glorious and great spirits"; and he urged Sir Charles "to remain with us until he dies ... that he may leave his noble, great and glorious spirit of harmony and love to all his medical brethren ... whether we call ourselves "British" or "Provincial" as long as his days are spared". The discussion continued and the motion was eventually defeated.

All through 1855 the scheming continued in the Metropolitan Branch, its suggested rule changes tending more and more towards allowing it to break altogether from its parent body and become an independent society. Lankester, while he agreed that some change was needed, opposed the more extreme moves. And so in August the time came for the Association's annual meeting in York, at which the Branch's proposals were again to be discussed. It was a poorly attended meeting, deliberately packed by the Worcester (Sir Charles's) Branch. A day and a half were spent in acrimonious discussion of London's suggestions and even scientific papers were crowded out of the time-table. Eventually the proposed change of name was defeated by a majority of 50 to 31 (out of a total Membership of 2,188), "although [it] was warmly and eloquently advocated by Dr. Lankester" and others. The whole of ·the second day was devoted to the suggested rule changes, and "much eloquence and ingenuity were spent on matters of no public interest, this giving a tedious character to the whole proceedings".

> The combatants continued the contest with untiring energy, the London party springing up with fresh vigour after every defeat, and disputing every inch of the ground with indomitable perseverence.

But the "cause was evidently hopeless from a strong muster of the Worcester party".[4]

However, there was considerable dissatisfaction among members over the matter of the name change. A number of branches, pointing out how small the attendance at the Annual Meeting had been, requisitioned a Special Meeting, which was held in Birmingham in November. In the interval a referendum among the whole membership approved the change by a large majority and Sir Charles, on mature consideration, also decided to give it his support. The opinions of most members were probably summed up in a very lengthy letter from "A Provincial" written to the *Lancet* during that interval. "Representing by no means the highest class of practitioners", he jibed:

> there was no justification in the Metropolitan Branch assuming to be the leading branch of the Association, and yet it has been playing the busybody throughout, and intermeddling in such a way as no other branch of the Association would have been guilty of.

And he accused the branch of aiming to dominate the Association to the extent of making it a "Metropolitan Association". Yet many paragraphs further on he wrote:

> The decision at York need not be regarded as final; the causes that influenced it are already in part obliterated; men may be led who will not be driven; innovations and improvements in old institutions, to be successful must be undertaken by those whose antecedents inspire confidence ... Much as we provincials would deprecate any attempt to convert us into a *Metropolitan* Association, we might not object to become a National one if our provincial rights were guaranteed.[5]

The militancy of a faction of the Metropolitan Branch had clearly raised unnecessary fears.

The Birmingham meeting was a lively one with no holds barred on either side, and at least one reporter from the medical press could not contain his glee. According to the *Medical Times and Gazette*, to which the scene was reminiscent of grand opera,

> Dr. Lankester, Mr. Ancell, Dr. Richardson and others, are discovered in various disguises, fabricating weapons of various kinds, to be used in the forthcoming conflict. The introductory chorus is characteristic of the heterogenous nature of the materials concerned, and the acrimony and fierceness of the approaching strife ... As every instrumentalist blows his own trumpet, or endeavours to play first fiddle, the ear is almost deafened by the tumult ... The chorus having been concluded, the serious business of the piece immediately commences, and one of the dark figures among the conspirators, who is supposed to be under Satanic influence, makes a long and violent speech ... denouncing vengeance against an enemy, whom ... he describes as approaching from the direction of the Malvern Hills. The evil genius of the British Metropolis, embodied in the person of Cerberus with three heads [Lankester's delegation], then commences a terrific howling ...
>
> While the tumult and confusion are raging on all sides, Sir Charles Hastings enters as the Wizard of Worcester ... and the noise is still further augmented; the clouds of darkness which hung over the scene grow still thicker; the Satanic delegate commences his speech anew; while Dr. Lankester, Dr. Richardson and Mr. Ancell, incorporated in the threefold Cerberus, all begin spouting at once some long speeches which they have learned beforehand ...
>
> But Sir Charles, who, at first, adopts a stern and forbidding aspect ... relaxes his features into a benignant smile, and at the same time waves his enchanted wand, when the effects upon the turbulent crowd before him [are immediate]. The clouds instantly disperse; the gloomy streets are magically changed into a splendidly illuminated banqueting hall; the music melts down into a soft allegretto movement.[6]

The writer concluded by apologizing for his levity, paying a glowing tribute to Sir Charles, and addressing the Association by its new name.

Thus, amid strife and conflict, did the PMSA give birth to that lusty infant, the British Medical Association (BMA), actively assisted by the attendant accoucheurs, Drs Lankester and Richardson and Mr. Ancell. Two years later the *Association Medical Journal* became the *British Medical Journal* (*BMJ*).

All through the gestation period of the BMA, both the PMSA and the latter's turbulent Metropolitan Counties Branch had been discussing with the Government the contents of the long overdue Medical Reform Bill. Numerous bills, mostly introduced by private members, had already been before Parliament and had been rejected because of the inability of the various medical bodies to agree, and the matter was now urgent. The PMSA had had a medical reform committee since 1837, and the Metropolitan Branch had, as we have seen, set up its own with Lankester in the Chair, at its foundation: Lankester was also a prominent member of the Association's Committee from at least 1854. His membership of these committees is the earliest record I have been able to find of his active participation in the reform movement, but by then he was in a position of authority; it therefore seems likely that he had been known and respected in reforming circles for some time before that; indeed, such was highly probable in view of his known antipathy to the stranglehold of the Royal Colleges. Perhaps he had been an individual member of the PMSA, or perhaps he had belonged to the London BMA, though if the latter, he would have found it difficult to reconcile his moderate views with the more radical outlook of that body.

From 1853 onwards Lankester played a leading role in the PMSA's fight for a Medical Reform Bill. He attended assiduously meetings of both the Branch and Association Reform Committees and, to judge by the frequency with which his name appears in reports of these meetings, he often spoke at them. Feeling among members was sharply divided between those who were prepared to concede almost everything in order to obtain a bill, and those who were only willing to meet the corporations part of the way. Lankester was one of the first group, and he is only reported on one occasion as refusing to accept a proposal insisted on by the Colleges. He argued vigorously for compromise at meeting after meeting. In one of these discussions, in 1857, he summarized the stark reality which members must face:

> Few persons, unless they lived in London, could form any idea of the power of the ruling body of these Colleges, not so much in their corporate capacity, as in that of individuals. They were the medical attendants of nearly every member of both Houses of Parliament, and they were frequently consulted by those members with regard to particular Bills which came before them. The Committee had, therefore, from time to time, felt it was quite impossible to pass a Bill against the Corporations, especially when the Government took up this position: "Unless you and the corporations agree, we will have nothing to do with you".

Referring to a particular meeting of the Committee with the Colleges he continued:

They [the Committee] did, he believed verily sell their consciences on that
occasion in order that they might get a bill. Well, that was a very
humiliating position to take, he owned, but they did it with this in view,
that they had better have that Bill than no bill at all. Anything would be
better than the state of chaos in which the profession now was.[7]

He was not, however, prepared to give in to the Colleges entirely
without a fight. For instance, the first time his activities as a reformer are
mentioned, he was chairing a meeting of the Branch Reform Committee
which was passing a motion urging all members to write to Members of
Parliament asking them to support a Branch deputation which was to visit
a minister. And on other occasions he frequently enjoined the virtues of
lobbying MPs, enlisting public support and similar actions.

In March, 1854, by which time the PMSA had been discussing its own
draft Bill for two years, its Reform Committee met to discuss the bill
currently before Parliament, that of Mr. Brady, one of the few medically
qualified MPs. It was a "little" bill, Lankester said, as opposed to their own
"great" bill, and could do nothing to bring about genuine reform. "If
medical men could only be united, it would be just as easy to pass a great
bill as a little bill. A strongly worded motion against Brady's bill was sent
to the Commons. A few days later Lankester led a delegation from the
Committee to see Lord Palmerston and stated bluntly, in opening the
discussion, that their intention was to object to Brady's bill. Palmerston
duly resisted its further progress and, instead, considered a draft of that
drawn up by the Association's Reform Committee.

In December the Committee approached Mr. Headlam, MP, and
obtained his parliamentary services on their behalf. After many
unavoidable delays, Mr. Headlam finally obtained an audience for them
with Sir George Gray, the Home Secretary, in May, 1855, when a large
deputation including Lankester and a number of MPs, presented Gray
with an address. Mr. Headlam introduced a Bill in June, but then Gray
delayed its further progress so that copies could be sent to the Colleges.
Making the most of this pause, the Association saw to it that Parliament
was inundated with petitions in favour of the Bill, from its own branches
and the public alike, and the Committee reported excitedly that they had
"the strongest reasons for stating that the replies sent by the Medical
Colleges to the enquiries of the Home Secretary showed a very decided
preponderance of opinion in favour of the Association Bill,"[8] though the
Universities were less favourably disposed. All this was reported and
discussed at the Annual Meeting in August, 1855, when the Committee
proposed that the Association should support the Bill through its second
reading. The Meeting adopted the report with enthusiasm, some members
being so optimistic about the speedy passage of the Bill that Lankester rose

to point out that only through their own continued efforts had they a chance of success, and that they must continue to lobby their MPs and use every other means of persuasion open to them. It was a long speech, and he continued with an account of the chaotic state of medical education, one of the problems which their Bill was designed to address. In particular, he railed against the College of Surgeons, which was proving the most obdurate of the corporations in coming to an agreement. He pointed out:

> that some of the Colleges were regarded as representatives of the profession. The College of Surgeons was consulted upon every occasion. What was the College of Surgeons doing? Never at any period in the history of the medical profession were they more loose in their examinations (Cheers). Recollect that a diploma could be obtained by men who had not studied more than nine months; and that diploma was looked on as affording a legitimate entrance to all positions which the Government had to bestow on the medical profession.[9]

In December, Lankester accompanied yet another delegation to Sir George Gray, but it came away "much disappointed", for Sir George was unable either to take over Headlam's Bill on behalf of the Government, or to expedite its progress through the House, there being too much other business. By now it was clear that the Association's optimism had been very premature.

Throughout 1856 their frustration continued, despite a barrage of petitions and deputations. In April matters were further complicated by Lord Elcho, who brought forward in the Lords a far more radical bill, ostensibly giving the Association (now the BMA, not the PMSA) almost all it was demanding; but the Association continued to support Mr. Headlam on the realistic grounds they had adopted all along - that the corporations would never allow the passage of a bill such as Lord Elcho's. One of the planks of Headlam's Bill was that a Council should be established as the ruling body for the whole profession, and the way in which its members would be chosen, which would obviously be of vital importance for the fair representation of the various classes of practitioner (physicians, surgeons and general practitioners), had been very carefully worked out. In May, a horrified leading article in the *AMJ* reported that a change had been made in the Bill which would allow the Government to appoint all the members of the Council, thus annulling the principle of direct or indirect representation of each class. The Editor hoped that the Reform Committee "would ponder long and deeply" before agreeing to such a change, and announced that he put his trust in that Committee, though by then he should have known them better.

For the truth was that the Royal Colleges had taken fright at Lord Elcho's Bill, and realized at last that they would have to make some concessions themselves in order to reach an agreement to their own best advantage. They had, therefore, formed a joint negotiating body to modify Headlam's already conciliatory Bill still further in their favour. By June the Bill had been redrafted to the advantage of the Colleges to such an extent that they considered it their own, and all the Reform Committee could do was to draft two reluctant resolutions summing up the situation as they saw it for consideration at the Annual Meeting at Birmingham on 29 July. The first resolution stated that the "provisions of the Bill ... carry out the principles of uniformity of examination and qualification, reciprocity of practice, and registration which the Association has always contended for". The other, moved by Lankester, read, "Without pledging themselves to every detail ... the Committee think its general provisions so beneficial ... that they are desirous of seeing the Bill at once passed into law".[10]

The atmosphere at the 1856 Annual Meeting was very different from that of 1855. The presentation of the Reform Committee's report was followed by an acrimonious discussion concerning representation on the proposed Council, and a number of members, including William Budd, opposed the Report strongly. They put forward an amendment, which Budd seconded, instructing the Committee to oppose the clause giving the Government the power to nominate the whole Council; it should be allowed one third at most. But the amendment was defeated and the original resolution adopted by a large majority.

Events in 1857 proceeded much as they had in 1856, with further changes to Headlam's Bill in favour of the corporations, further concessions on the part of the Reform Committee, delegations and deputations, in all of which Lankester played a conspicuous part. Lord Elcho introduced another radical Bill. However, on 13 May, Headlam's Bill was given its first reading in Parliament. It proposed that the governing Council should be composed of seventeen persons chosen by the corporations and six nominated by the Crown. Clauses ensured that the Colleges retained almost all their traditional powers, even that to license practitioners who had never studied surgery; university graduates wishing to practise as physicians would still have to sit that College's examinations. Despite this, the Metropolitan Branch was advised by Lankester to accept the Bill with four provisos, one of which concerned the choice of members of the Council and another, for obvious personal reasons, the need for graduates to be licenced by the College of Physicians. At its July meeting, the Branch elected Lankester its President.

Headlam's Bill was approved by a comfortable majority at its Second Reading on 1 July, but it then came up against the hazard of all Private Member's bills and ran out of time, the Government still refused to take it up, and Headlam dropped it. This was the situation when the Reform Committee presented its Report to the Association's Annual Meeting at Nottingham on 28 July, 1857, and, as in 1856, the Meeting was a heated one. There was much argument between those who would go to any lengths to obtain a bill, and others whose willingness to compromise was strictly limited. Once again, William Budd was among the more vociferous of those who rose to attack the Committee. Among many points made in a long speech, he felt that the Committee had put the Association "in a false position by advocating in an unflinching manner a Bill which ... was so surcharged with corporation interests as to render it impossible of acceptance by any liberal ministers of this country".[11] He proposed what was virtually a motion of no confidence in the Committee and, suggesting that it needed new blood, put forward the names of four new, and presumably militant, members. The Committee gladly accepted them and co-opted Budd as well.

Then Lankester rose to defend the Committee's actions, while fully acknowledging the truth of Budd's remarks. The Committee was well aware from the beginning, he said, that no bill would get through Parliament without the consent of the Royal Colleges, and its members knew that the Surgeons were utterly opposed to the Association's original draft of its Bill, and the Physicians cool towards it, while the Government had stated flatly that unless the BMA and the Colleges agreed, no further notice would be taken of the former. The Committee had then sought a meeting with the Committee of the Colleges, and it was at that meeting that they "did verily sell their consciences" in order to get a bill. Possibly, he suggested, the whole matter should be shelved and a Royal Commission appointed.

At this point Sir Charles Hastings, the President of the BMA's Council, announced that he had just that moment received a message from William Cowper, the President of the Board of Health, saying that he would himself be introducing a Medical Reform Bill in the next session of Parliament, and wished to consult Sir Charles. Once again passions were let loose. Lankester pointed out hidden meanings in Cowper's statement, Dr. Stewart expressed total lack of faith in the Medical Reform Committee, the suggested Royal Commission was supported and opposed, and it was found necessary to propose that the meeting proceed to next business (a paper reading session) in order to separate the combatants. Lankester's scientific contribution to the Meeting was a long paper on human entozoa (worms). He was elected one of two Vice-Chairmen of the Association, and in proposing a toast at the Dinner he took the opportunity to suggest that the BMA should make some attempt at a rational timetable for its meetings, as the British Association did, for at present they were an inextricable tangle of science and business. He found it neccesary to return to this complaint for several successive years.

In February, 1858, when all seemed set for Cowper's Bill, Palmerston's government fell and Lord Derby became Prime Minister, leaving Cowper once more a private member; but despite this, he decided to press on with his Bill. This time he enlisted the help of John Simon, the Medical Officer to the Board of Health, and together they drafted a bill which included most of the BMA's requirements. Naively, both the BMA and the *Lancet* supported it, and on 15 May a very large deputation from the BMA, led by Sir Charles Hastings and including both Budd and Lankester among its members, "waited upon the Right Honorable Spencer Walpole, Secretary of State for the Home Department, for the purpose of enlisting his support and that of the Government" for the Bill. In the discussion, Budd emphasized that the proposed Council should not only fix the standard of education, but have the power to enforce it; and Lankester wished to ensure that all doctors were qualified in both medicine and surgery. But all through April the corporations had been in conference with Lord Derby as well as with Walpole, petitioning against the Bill.

By the time Cowper's Bill came up for its Second Reading on 2 June confusion reigned in Parliament, for Lord Elcho had introduced his third bill, and Thomas Wakley, editor of the *Lancet* and radical Member for Finchley, had produced another. However, Cowper's Bill eventually went to Committee where Members were subjected to intense pressure from the Colleges, which used all their own members' professional and social leverage to water it down, attacking in particular the proposed Council in the form and with the powers suggested. Needless to say, the Colleges were victorious and they won, not through parliamentary debate, but by lobbying Walpole. The Council was deprived of all authority to define courses of study or appoint its own examiners, and the powers of the Colleges remained virtually intact. In addition, a stipulation that the six Council members appointed by the Crown should not be officers of the Colleges or Universities was dropped, as was the clause requiring practitioners to be qualified in both medicine and surgery. Only the establishment of a unified register of practitioners, and the recognition that those so registered might practise anywhere in the United Kingdom, remained intact. When the Bill received its Third Reading on 9 July, the victory of the Royal Colleges was almost complete.

The day after the passing of the Bill, the Metropolitan Branch, whether by coincidence or in gratitude for his labours is not known, elected Lankester as their delegate to the General Council of the Association. His last action on medical reform seems to have been at a Branch Meeting in October, when there was a long discussion on the need for the chairman of the governing Council, to be created under the Act, to be a medical man. He ended the discussion by pointing out that:

> the Act had been promoted by the BMA for the purpose of protecting the profession against the Colleges, and that a layman might do this better than a medical man. He also felt that the public might benefit from a lay president. [12]

The following year, under the terms of the Bill, the Royal College of Physicians abolished its Extra-Licence, the holders automatically being granted full membership. From that time on Lankester, having fought so hard to remove his long-standing grievance against the College, signed himself "MRCP".

His intervention in the great reform debate had been both sustained and influential. He believed passionately in the need for regulation of his profession but was prepared to compromise to achieve it; this he always and consistently admitted. Yet he never quietly submitted to the dictates of the corporations - it was always he who organized the mass petitions and lobbying of MPs, and he was a member of almost every delegation to ministers. He was unstinting in the time he was prepared to give to the cause for six years, despite the fact that half way through the fight, he was appointed to the new and demanding post of Medical Officer of health for St. James's, Westminster, with its enormous responsibilities. To what extent he moulded the BMA's policy after his own ideas it is impossible to say, but there is no doubt that the majority of its members could always be counted on to follow his line. In view of his prominence in the struggle, together with the leading part he played in the transformation of the PMSA to the BMA, it is strange that neither his obituaries nor his long entry in the *Dictionary of National Biography*, make any mention of him in either context.

Chapter Eight

Interlude 1855-1857

Between 1850 and 1854 Lankester published very little and, apart from his work for the British Association and the beginning of his joint editorship of the *Quarterly Journal of Microscopical Science*, his activities as a naturalist were in abeyance. In 1855, however, a book on the natural history of Deeside appeared under his editorship, thanks to the good offices of his friend Sir James Clark, Physician to the Queen.[1] Sir James (1788-1870) was a much travelled Scot, one of whose interests was the effect of climate on tuberculosis. He had practised for some years in Rome, and during the summer used to attend wealthy British patients visiting the mineral springs of Germany. In due course he became Physician to Prince Leopold of Belgium, then to the Duchess of Kent and, on her accession to the throne, to Queen Victoria herself, a post which he occupied with integrity despite making one famous mistake.*[2] He was a great friend of the Royal Family, and it was he who recommended that they should purchase Balmoral because of its excellent soil and climate.[3] Unexpectedly for a man in such privileged circumstances, he was a strong advocate of medical reform and highly critical of the Government for consulting only the Royal Colleges on the future regulation of the profession, so excluding the general practitioners from any say in their own future.[4] It may have been through their mutual interest in that highly contentious matter that he and Lankester were drawn together.

When the Royal Family was in residence at Balmoral, Sir James lived at nearby Birkhall, where he was in the habit of entertaining his friends; so that it would have been there that, some time in 1854, he invited Lankester to stay, and during the visit introduced his guest to Prince Albert. The Prince had recently acquired the manuscript of a book entitled *The Natural History of Deeside and Braemar* by William McGillivray, Professor of Natural History at Aberdeen University, who had died before his work could be published. As it dealt with the countryside immediately adjacent

---

* He diagnosed the Queen's Lady-in-waiting, Lady Flora Hastings, as being pregnant when she was, in fact, suffering from an abdominal tumour.

to Balmoral the Prince, with his well-known interest in natural science, was anxious that it should be published, and who better to see it through the press than Lankester, with his wide knowledge of natural history and his many contacts in the world of science? He readily agreed to edit the book. According to his preface it needed a great deal of work, from drastic pruning to revision of each section by the appropriate specialist, and he obtained a galaxy of the best known scientists to undertake the job. Many, such as Sir William Jardine, Nathaniel Ward and Edward Forbes (shortly before his untimely death), were his own friends; others, such as Sir William Hooker of Kew, were recruited by Clark,[5] part of the latter's "constant and important assistance" acknowledged by Lankester. The only addition to the book made by the Editor was a short section on red deer, which he compiled mainly from the answers to a questionnaire sent to a dozen local land-owners, game-keepers and foresters. The book was published by command of the Queen for private circulation only, and the Prince presented an inscribed copy to the Garden Library at Frogmore[6] (Fig. 30).*

In 1856, two years after the Broad Street cholera outbreak, Lankester published the results of the observations on the well waters of the district which he had undertaken at the time, including drawings of the fungus which had clouded the water from the fatal pump[9] (Fig. 31). He did not identify the organism, and except that it was a flagellate fungus, probably belonging to the genus *Pythium*, it is impossible to do so now. The paper continued with the description of another fungus found more recently as a surface mat on well water from Cirencester, but as this water had been stored in an open tank for a fortnight, it is perhaps not surprising that contamination had occurred.

Lankester was much interested in the biology of water at this time. There was a current fashion for aquavivaria in the home, and it was a subject on which he had previously written an article for the *English Cyclopaedia*; now he enlarged this into a book, *The Aquavivarium, Fresh and Marine, being an account of the principles and objects involved in the domestic culture of water plants and animals* (1856). Lankester, ever the educator, ended his preface with the hope that his remarks "will in some manner contribute to make the prevailing taste for establishing domestic aquavivaria subservient to the teaching of Natural History and a study of God's works". He mentioned that the source of the idea was Nathaniel Ward's closed cases for growing plants, gave a simple scientific explanation of the balance of plant and animal life in water, and then

---

* It was probably this episode which led to the belief in the Lankester family that Edwin had been tutor in botany to the royal children,[7] an idea for which there is no confirmation in the Royal Archives at Windsor Castle.[8]

This Work,

PRINTED BY COMMAND OF

THE QUEEN,

is presented to

The Garden Library, Frogmore.

BY

H.R.H. PRINCE ALBERT.

Fig. 30. Fly-leaf of the Royal Family's copy of *The Natural History of Braemar*.

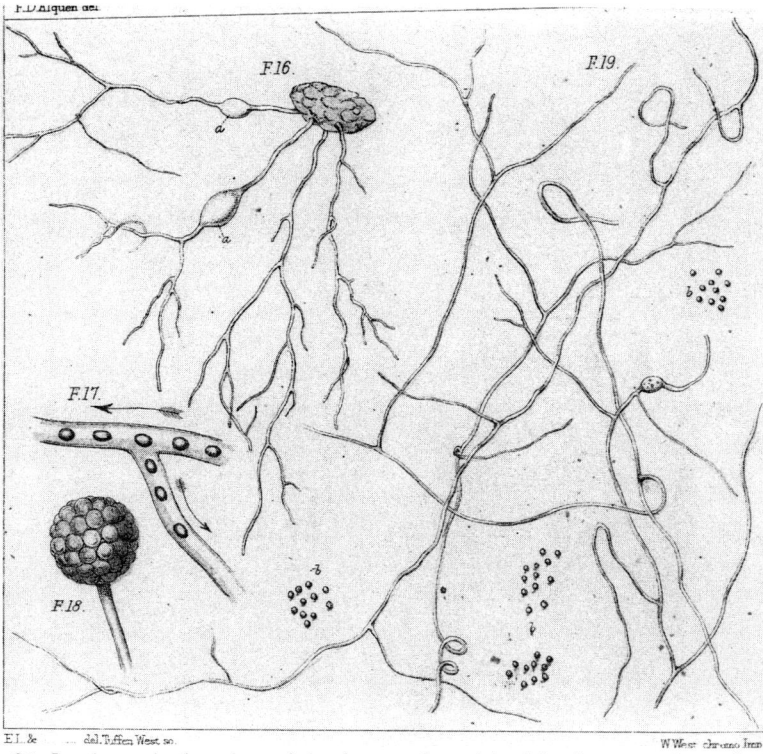

Fig. 31. Lankester's drawing of the fungus found by him in water from the Broad Street pump.

Fig. 32. No. 192, Piccadilly, the premises of Robert Hardwicke, in 1840. The old Vestry Hall of St. James's Church is visible at the extreme left.

Fig. 33. Robert Hardwicke, publisher.

proceeded to the practical details of setting up an aquavivarium, of which he had obviously had first hand experience.

The Aquavivarium was the first of Lankester's books to be published by Robert Hardwicke who, at the time, had just moved his premises from 26, Duke Street to 192, Piccadilly, only a few steps from St. James's Church (Fig. 32): indeed, the book had been written at the publisher's request.

Robert Hardwicke (1822-1875) (Fig. 33) was the younger brother of William Hardwicke (1817-1881), Lankester's fellow student at University College (Chapter 2). Robert had followed his brother to London from their Lincolnshire home, had been apprenticed to a printer and publisher, and had eventually set up on his own, specializing more and more in medical and biological books.[10] He doubtless benefitted considerably from William's medical connections, and it must have been his brother who introduced Lankester to him. Robert took a very practical interest in his authors and their activities, helping a number of them on their first steps to success, and it was by no means unusual for him to suggest subjects on which they might write, to his own advantage as well as their's. His association with Edwin and Phebe Lankester was to be a long one.

Edwin's fame as a lecturer was not confined to the metropolis. On 23 September, 1856, he was invited to speak at a joint meeting of five West Midlands field clubs, the Worcestershire, Malvern, Woolhope, Cotswold and Warwickshire, which was "holden" at the rooms of the first named, his subject being "The Natural Sciences as a branch of education and a means of national wealth". Unfortunately he had a bad cold, and started by apologizing for hoarseness and depression, but despite this, the Worcestershire Society reported that he gave "an extremely interesting and eloquent extemporaneous address" lasting upwards of an hour. He discussed each of the natural sciences in turn, and emphasized his belief that the only answer to the problem of the mystery of life was that "God made it so", a remark which was received with tumultous applause. As to his hobby-horse, the need to include natural history in the education of every citizen, he suggested that the Worcestershire Naturalists could help by starting classes for the local boys.[11]

The talk was such a success that Lankester was asked to speak at a similar function the following year, which he did on his way home from a holiday in the Welsh mountains. This time he spoke "On the domestication of water plants" and gave a description of the pleasures of vivaria, which "he believed had not yet penetrated to Worcestershire", with instructions on setting them up. Once again he ended with a plea for the teaching of natural history, a subject to which he returned in his speech after the "Collation", this time emphasizing "the great value of enlisting in its cause the sympathies of the ladies".[12]

One of the series of letters which Phebe Lankester wrote to John Forster in 1889 (Chapter 5), many years after her husband's death, about her memories of Charles Dickens, concerned the Dickens family's amateur theatricals. In particular, she remembered Wilkie Collins' play, *The Frozen Deep*, which the family put on in 1857. They had been mounting plays since 1844, but when they moved to Tavistock House, Tavistock Square, in 1855, Dickens opened his own small theatre there in which he, his family and friends undertook all their own management, production and acting. The following year the family went on holiday to Boulogne, a favourite spot, accompanied by Collins, and it was during that holiday that Collins wrote his melodrama for the next Dickens production. Its first performance was in the Tavistock Theatre on 6 January, 1857, and it was a huge success, attracting an audience of 100 strong. It was presumably of this that Phebe wrote in 1889:

... my recollections of the Play of the "Frozen Deep" which was performed *first* in the house of Chas Dickens in Tavistock Square. I and my husband were there, and some very distinguished people - I sat by Thackeray at supper, and heard Lord Campbell propose the health of our host. That evening was a very memorable one to me. I was *very* young, not long married and remember my dear husband saying to me, "When you are an old lady you will like to recall this evening". Alas! I am now *alone* to do so! I have no dates by me as to the year in which the "Frozen Deep" was produced.

And she asked again and again, in this and subsequent letters: "Please write again and give me the dates which I lack", something which Forster never seems to have done. Her unease about the dating of her memories so long after the event (she would have been 64 when her letter was written), was well-founded, for in 1857 she was 32 years old and had been married for twelve years, hardly a "*very* young" married woman. Given that both her recollections are true, perhaps the answer is that she and Edwin had first been invited to the Dickens amateur theatricals after that summer holiday in 1849, when they had only been married for four years and, after so long an interval, she was confusing this with the later performance of the "Frozen Deep". Only a year after the success of that play, which was put on on many other occasions for benefit performances for various charities, Dickens separated from his wife, Catherine. Of this Phebe wrote to Forster:

I knew Charles Dickens well, until after his separation from his wife - *she* I knew after that event - but we saw him only seldom.

It seems that she and Edwin took Catherine's part in the sad affair.[13]

Chapter Nine

Medical Officer Of Health   1856-1873

When on 10 January, 1856, Lankester took up his post as Medical Officer of Health (MOH) for St. James's, Westminster, he was already a busy man. He terminated his appointment at the Royal Pimlico Dispensary, but he was still lecturing at the Grosvenor Place School and at New College, was Medical Officer to the English Widows' Fund, and had at least some private practice. Among his voluntary occupations he was in the thick of the struggle for the Medical Reform Bill, which was at its height, and he had kept on several of his scientific posts.

His first action as MOH was to draw up his own job description (the Vestry having already admitted that it did not know what the post would entail), and to this end he and the other newly appointed Medical Officers consulted with John Simon, Medical Officer to the Government Board of Health. By 23 January, Lankester was able to submit to his Vestry certain definite proposals. Its aim, he said, should be to reduce by half the present death rate in the parish so as to bring it down to the average for the country, for to save life meant to produce wealth. 400 deaths meant at least 4,000 sick, and therefore expensive, persons. To reach this target, the MOH must be able to obtain basic information from all available sources; the Vestry itself must supply him with weekly returns of births and deaths; institutions, hospitals, doctors and parsons must report to him any incipient epidemics that came to their notice; and an Inspector of Nuisances (or Sanitary Inspector) must be able to visit regularly every house in the parish and report on it on a standard form. In return, the MOH would lay a fortnightly report before the Vestry and would write a comprehensive annual report. He ended by requesting a room or office from which to work, and suggested that all parishioners should be notified of his appointment.

All, or most of these proposals must have been accepted, including the appointment of a sanitary inspector, one James Morgan, who submitted his own reports to the Vestry, separately from Lankester's, from 1860. Despite the fact that Lankester's was only a part time appointment, he met Morgan every morning to "receive from him a report of the previous day's work, and then give him directions for the work of the day."[1] The role of the sanitary inspectors, though they underwent no formal training, was crucial, for the slum landlords, some of whom might also be vestrymen, would rarely admit to a nuisance unless forced to, and their tenants were much too frightened to inform on them; house-to-house visitation by a third party was the only way the requisite information could be obtained.

There had been much speculation, some of it light-hearted but only partly tongue-in-cheek, about the salaries which would be offered to men with the qualities required of the future MOH:

> A man must not only be an accomplished physician, but he must also be a chemist, toxicologist, something of an engineer, an astronomer, architect, a natural philosopher in the widest sense; he must, besides, have something of the undertaker about him, and should, moreover, be triply contagion-proof ... as he would on average inhale the emanations of typhus and smallpox for at least twelve hours out of the twenty-four. We are curious to see what the salary of such a universal genius will be.

Just before the appointment of the Officers the *Lancet*, in a leading article, noted that it had been influentially stated that their salary should not exceed £400. The journal was shocked, insisting that it should "be suited to a gentleman of position and education"[2]. As we have seen, Lankester had been appointed to his part-time post at a salary of just £100 until such time as his functions should become clearer. In the richest parish in London he continued at this salary without complaint until July, 1857, when he detailed at length to the Vestry the huge amount of work which fell to his lot, and asked for a rise. But the Vestry, pointing out that it had appointed a Surveyor to assist him, and that he had held the post for only 18 months, postponed a decision until the end of the year. In January, 1858, they doubled his salary to £200, and it appears to have remained at this figure until his death in 1874. Despite the *Lancet*'s ideas on the matter, this was quite consistent with the salaries of other metropolitan Officers, some of whom were paid even less.

Up to the end of 1859 Lankester's fortnightly reports, together with the discussions arising therefrom and any action taken, were written up in the Vestry Minutes. For an account of his stewardship up to that date, therefore, I have been able to draw both on those Minutes and on his Annual Reports. However, at the end of 1859 a Sanitary Committee was set up with delegated powers, resulting in little further mention of public health matters in the Vestry Minutes: my account from then on is therefore drawn entirely from the Annual Reports.

These Reports are methodical, thorough, detailed and hard hitting. Lankester did not play down the horrors of life in the Berwick Street slums, but neither did he exaggerate them. At the beginning of each

Report the year's overall statistics were set out in neatly tabulated form, the subject matter of the tables being determined by the most pressing events of the year. These were followed by separate sections in which subjects of particular interest were discussed in depth and action either reported on or urged. Lankester knew that the only way he would get the maximum cooperation from his Vestry was through its pocket, and to this end the first three pages of his first Report were devoted entirely to showing his employers how much money they would save by spending on sanitary measures. For instance, of the 1854 cholera epidemic he wrote:

> If we take into consideration the value of four hundred and fifty lives, the cost of funerals, the attendance on the dying, as well as on the sick who recovered, and also of the loss arising from the flight of those lodging in the cholera district, almost depopulating it, the lowest estimate of the cost, to the parish ... would give the sum of nearly £100,000. It is by calculations such as this that the enormous cost of disease and death can alone be estimated ... and that any estimate can be formed of the reckless extravagance of a neglect of sanitary arrangements, and of the immense economy of an effective system of sanitary organisation.[3]

And again:

> ... one of the most profitable investments of capital is in the health of a community of working men. This principle is so clearly apprehended in the treatment of working animals, that it would scarcely be necessary to mention it were it not neglected in the treatment of human beings.[4]

We have learned enough of Lankester to be certain that he was no hard-faced businessman, as these passages and many others in his Reports would imply, but rather a realist who was well aware of his employers' priorities and fully prepared to exploit them, if that meant loosening their purse strings while retaining their respect and cooperation for further expenditures. Of course, it was by no means always that he got his way, and then he would hammer on at the same evil year after year, and if the money were eventually granted would bestow on his audience his praises for their generosity and statesmanship. Occasionally, when the Vestry blocked a measure on which he felt particularly strongly, he did not hesitate to speak his mind, but on the whole he seems to have managed his masters with consumate skill, keeping their interest in the health of the parish and their respect for himself, while cajoling as much money from them as was in any way possible. Of that first pioneering group of medical officers of health, some kept on the right side of their vestries by treating the job as a sinecure and spending practically nothing, but others were as devoted and energetic as was Lankester. A number of the latter, however, found their vestries far more obstructive than he, and one cannot help suspecting that these men had not Lankester's charm and guile.

The parish of St. James's, Westminster, was bounded on the north by Oxford Street, on the south by Pall Mall, on the east by Wardour Street, and on the west by Regent Street, Burlington Arcade and Green Park (Fig. 14). It was a royal parish, and one of the richest in London, as Lankester constantly reiterated. But it was also an extraordinary parish, with all the wealth concentrated in the southernmost St. James's Square Division. The Berwick Street Division in the north, which included the infamous Broad Street, contained the densest population and the worst overcrowding in the whole of London. In between these two, both geographically and in population density, lay the Golden Square Division, where not so long ago Lankester had lodged with Edward Forbes. The first table of Lankester's first Annual Report gave a stark picture of conditions in the parish.

District	Population 1851	Population per acre	No. of deaths in 1856
St. James's Sq. Div.	11469	134	137
Golden Sq. Div.	14139	262	317
Berwick St. Div.	10798	432	228

The very high death rate in the Golden Square Division was due to the presence there of the workhouse, containing 600 persons; if the 106 deaths there were excluded, then the number of deaths per thousand in the Golden Square Division was 13, in the St. James's Square Division, 12, but in the Berwick Street Division, 25. He went on to tabulate the main causes of death; first the "zymotic" diseases, comprising smallpox, measles, scarlet fever and hooping cough (sic), diarrhoea and typhus, which between them killed 85 people, scarlet fever and hooping cough being by far the most lethal; then "phthsis" (consumption, tuberculosis), causing 110 deaths; and finally "various forms of inflammatory diseases of the lungs", which were responsible for 138 deaths. These three groups of diseases, accounting for 343 deaths in all, were responsible for half the total deaths in the parish.

Following in the steps of William Farr, Lankester used statistics frequently and forcefully throughout his tenure of the post of MOH, though inevitably he handled figures in a far less sophisticated manner than would be the case today. He often compared averages, and sometimes "cases per thousand", but he never used percentages. He knew the importance of working with the largest samples obtainable, and he compared many different parameters, from the three divisions of his parish to the effect of height above sea level.

While discussing the death rate in the St. James's Square Division, he made special mention of the one black spot there, the Burlington Arcade, which at that time must have been roofed with some opaque material. The houses over the shops were inhabited both by families and by young shop workers, the rooms were tiny and extremely badly ventilated, and the death rate was high. Lankester requested the Government to allow ventilation through the dead wall on the west side of Burlington House: "My application was, however, peremptorily refused". It was not until two years later, and futher agitation on Lankester's part, that the Arcade was reroofed with glass, making it so much lighter that the inhabitants had to burn far less gas, thus using up less oxygen, and the government allowed ventilation through the dead wall.

Lankester's main preoccupation, however, was with the sanitary condition of the houses of the poorer classes.

> It is not uncommon to find twenty or thirty persons living in a single house; and in one house in Peter Street, as many as fifty persons were found sleeping nightly in it, each floor, and sometimes each room, being occupied by one family. In the majority of cases these houses have been built for the acommodation of but one family.
>
> The worst feature, however, of the over-crowding in this parish is the very common practice of residence in cellars or kitchens ... in the majority of cases in which this occupation occurs, the places are quite unfit for human residence, and are such as are interdicted under the Nuisances Removal Act.[3]

By 1858 the kitchens* had indeed been cleared, but the landlords had begun to relet them. Here, and often in his reports, Lankester pleaded for the clearance of such premises, but he was only too well aware of what would happen to the evicted families: "If the people were sent to the neighbouring parishes they would only increase over-crowding there; and if they were sent to the suburbs, they would be removed from their work and become pauperised,"[5] for they could not afford transport to work. So both in his Annual Reports and in papers read to professional societies, he argued that overcrowding was the lesser evil, and that eviction should not be resorted to until such time as there was somwhere convenient for the people to go. There was a model lodging house in the parish, Ingestre Buildings, which housed 300 families and in which overcrowding was

---

* the kitchens of these erstwhile prosperous houses would have been in the basements

forbidden; there, there were no problems of excessive disease, and Lankester pleaded again and again for the slums to be torn down and more such establishments built in their place, but in this matter he never moved his Vestry. Overcrowding in the Berwick Street Division was as severe at his death as it had been when he took office.

Overcrowding raised another problem in the parish. There was no mortuary or "death house", so that when there was a death in a family, the body had to be kept among the living in the crammed rooms until such time as it could be buried. Neither, of course, was there anywhere convenient in which post mortems could be performed. In 1864 Lankester approached the Board of Guardians on the matter and obtained its backing for a request to the Vestry, but at the end of the year "the question was still in abeyance", though William Farr himself, in an appendix to the Registrar-General's Annual Report that year, had recommended:

> the construction of decent dead houses in every town through-out the kingdom. These structures are very much wanted in the neighbourhood of London, where scenes of the most disgusting kind are constantly enacted on account of the refusal of anyone to take in bodies found dead.

One of Lankester's earliest considerations for improving the health of the populace was to attend to the state of the drains which, he said, were often in a worse state in the wealthier parts of the parish than in the poorer, and he was astonished at the lack of complaints about the foul stench they emitted.

> The majority of houses have brick drains which, from age, have fallen away, and the soil has been permeated in every direction with the refuse from the sinks and water-closets. It has been not unfrequently the case that attention has been directed to such cases by the occurrence of fever, or other disease, which is invariably found more prevalent and fatal where such a state of things exists.[4]

Chadwick advocated abolishing the old open sewers and the building of closed ones, which would be kept sanitary by constant flushing out with large quantities of fresh water, and would discharge into the nearest river. Lankester, while recognizing the advantages of closed sewers, wondered where sufficient water for flushing them would come from, and realized that the pollution of the Thames had to be stopped. To this end he first advocated the continued use of open sewers, and later the ventilation of covered ones by means of tall, vertical pipes to carry off the noxious gases over the heads of the population. Needless to say, neither of these solutions was adopted. As to the pollution of the Thames, he followed

Chadwick in supporting strongly the idea of the German chemist, von Liebig, that the (uncomposted) output of the sewers might be used as fertilizer by the surrounding farms. At times he was strangely impractical.

A companion problem to the drains was the huge number of cesspools either under the houses or in their areas, often only detectable by their smell. Lankester does not state how many there were in the parish when he took office, but there must have been a few hundred, for despite an energetic programme of removal in 1856 and 1857, there were still 64 left in 1858. When it came to their clearance, it is surprising to read that "in no instance where improvements in drainage, and the removal of cesspools have been found necessary, has there been any occasion to resort to legal proceedings".[3] In view of the miserly reputation of the landlords this must be a tribute to Lankester's charm and persuasiveness, though it may also have had something to do with fear that the diseases so rife in the slums could one day spread to attack the St. James's Square Division with equal severity. Whatever the reason for the property owners' cooperation, Lankester's remarks could have done his cause no harm in the eyes of his employers, as he had doubtless calculated when he made them.

The presence of an astonishing number of the larger domestic animals constituted another major nuisance to the inhabitants of central London at the time. Because of transport difficulties, stables, cow-houses and slaughter-houses abounded, most of the last two, at least, being crammed into the already densely packed slums. In 1859 there were 392 stables in the parish, housing 1057 horses, and 901 people lived either over the stables or over their associated coach-houses. Manure was often piled high in huge stacks rather than carted away. All the premises were inspected during the year and 208 nuisances dealt with, it being easier, Lankester reported, to persuade the owners that filth was bad for their beasts than it was to persuade landlords that it was bad for their tenants.

As to the cow-houses,

There are eleven in the parish, all situate in the most populous districts ... In many instances I found the cow-houses in a very filthy condition, with insufficient ventilation, and no regularity observed in the removal of refuse necessarily accumulating from the animals. Some of them are under dwelling-houses, and, where this is the case, the inhabitants complain greatly of the stench produced.[3]

Two years later he was more specific. 205 cows were kept in the parish:

The nuisance of the cow-houses in Marshall Street is notorious throughout the whole parish; whatever may be done by the proprietor of this place, nothing can prevent the herding together of 25 or 30 cows in a room of a dwelling-house, in a row of other houses, from being a nuisance to all who may live near.[7]

In February of that year the Vestry wrote to the Cow-keepers' Association about the problem, and the Association replied that it would like an interview with the Board of Guardians as it disagreed with its orders about the width of stall to be allowed for each pair of cows. "I beg to say", added its Secretary ingratiatingly, "that your Board would have no cause to complain of the respectability of the delegation". Soon after taking office, Lankester put the cow-houses under inspection and organized regular removal of refuse but, as he said, "nothing ... can be done to render them unobjectionable, as long as they exist surrounded by houses, to the inhabitants of which they must act as a chronic nuisance".

He personally examined and compared specimens of milk from each cow-house and from the countryside, measuring their specific gravity with a "lactometer", leaving them to stand for 24 hours to determine the cream content, and finally, following Hassall's lead, submitting each specimen to direct microscopic examination, though without either concentrating or staining it. Amazingly he found no major faults, though most of the town milks were of poorer quality than that from the country. Eventually he obtained the Vestry's support, first for licensing the cow-houses, and then for abolishing them altogether, and by 1863 he was able to announce the closure of the last one.

There was no public abattoire in the parish, hence the need for the butchers to slaughter their animals themselves on their own premises, a common practice in Victorian Britain, but very objectionable in the crowded cities. In 1856 a new Act of Parliament required that all slaughter-houses should be licensed, and Lankester was asked by the Vestry's Paving and Nuisances Committee to draw up a report on the situation in the parish. This he presented on 4 October, and by 16 October the Vestry had already begun to act. It granted licences to only 17 of the 25 applicants, and these were put under inspection. Lankester proposed that they were given a code of regulations which, if not strictly adhered to, would result in the withdrawal of the licence. The number of slaughter-houses was further reduced in 1858, when only nine of the 31 applications were granted and underground premises were outlawed. But Lankester always held that slaughter-houses were less of a problem than stables and cow-houses, provided they were kept clean and detritus was removed regularly.

The water supply remained a major problem in London and, as might be expected of him, its improvement was one of Lankester's prime interests as MOH. In the parish of St. James's, Westminster, some water was supplied by two commercial companies, and some, despite the experiences of 1854, was still obtained from wells, including that in Broad Street.

> The two water companies furnish the houses by means of pipes communicating with the main, and water is turned on for a limited period during the twenty-four hours, except on the Sunday, when a period of forty-eight hours elapses. The water is stored in cisterns and butts. The use of water-butts is objectionable, as they are made of wood, and liable to decay.[3] (Fig. 21).

The Vestry went in perpetual fear of another outbreak of cholera, and on 9 October, 1857, after the disease had appeared again in Europe, the vestrymen asked Lankester to prepare a report on its possible recurrence in their parish: a week later he read his findings to them. That part of the report which concerned the sewers was promptly forwarded to the Metropolitan Board of Works, and a large committee was set up to confer with Lankester. His first request was that all the pumps should be locked, as the wells could all be contaminated from adjacent waterclosets. To back this up he wrote to John Simon, Medical Officer to the General Board of Health, and to all his fellow metropolitan MOH, asking for their opinion. To a man they backed him. He submitted their replies to the Vestry, and all are printed in that year's Annual Report. But so devoted were the vestrymen to the sparkling waters of their wells that the Committee defeated the motion to close them by the casting vote of the Chairman. It was, however, agreed that Lankester should draw up printed leaflets of health instructions which would be circulated to the whole parish and that, in the event of an outbreak, he should supervise house-to-house visitations. The Vestry adopted its Committee's report with the proviso that it should reconsider the question of the closure of the pumps and, though it took its time, the Cholera Committee did finally reverse its decision. As soon as the cholera scare was over, the pumps were unlocked!

In May, 1858, the Lancet, in a leading article, "War to the pump", quoted Lankester's views at length; resignedly the writer commented, "No doubt prejudice will have its way for some time to come, and men will swear by the pump their ancestors used"; but he ended, "The London 'cow with the iron tail' is pregnant with the elements of death". Continuing his attack on the pumps, Lankester reported to the Association for the Promotion of Social Science in 1860 that he had "in vain urged upon the authorities the closure of these pumps". In the 1866 London cholera outbreak there were 15 deaths in the parish, and now he sounded a note of real alarm and warned his Vestry yet again that "I dare not take the responsibility of remaining quiet while these pumps are open, and, at the risk of offending you by my pertinacity, I implore you to order the pumps

to be shut". At last his appeals seem to have been heard, for there is no
further mention of pumps in his Annual Reports.

Still pursuing his goal of a well informed public, he produced that year
a small book, *Cholera, what it is and how to prevent it*, in which he explained
in layman's terms his own ideas on how the disease was spread, and
described the preventive measures which should be taken by individuals
and by the authorities. The *Lancet* regarded the book as being just what
was needed to instruct the public so that it could help itself in the fight
against the disease. The volume is of considerable interest in that is shows
clearly Lankester's innate conservatism in scientific matters, a
conservatism which would cause him repeatedly to hedge his bets
between old ideas and new in that age of truly revolutionary scientific
discovery. A strong body of commercial opinion was, for its own
purposes, trying to convince the authorities that cholera was not a
contagious disease (the word "contagious" being used here more in the
sense in which we would use "infectious"). Concerning this, Lankester
wrote:

> It has been the entire failure of any other theory to account for the spread of
> cholera that inquirers have been drawn to accept the theory that the disease
> is contagious, and that it is only propagated by a poison which being
> generated in one body is communicated to another.

Acting on this premise, precautions must include the removal of all dirt
and filth. But he continued:

> All the evidence on which we rely for proving that cholera is a contagious
> disease, points to the evacuations of the patient as containing the poison
> germs ... These germs although more easily communicated through the
> agency of water, can undoubtedly be received through the air.

And aerial spread, he wrote, included infection via dirty water-closets.
Thus Lankester, while fully accepting Snow's theory of the water-borne
spread of the disease, could not entirely give up the traditional
"miasmata" theory, and while urging every effort to ensure the purity of
drinking water, as exemplified by his efforts to close the pumps, he
continued to insist that the cleaning and disinfection of drains was also of
paramount importance. Of the two methods for purifying drinking water
which he suggested house-holders themselves could undertake, one was
to boil all drinking water, but the other, to filter the water through a
flower-pot, would tragically have done more harm than good.

Water remained one of his chief preoccupations during his whole
tenure of the post of MOH. He agitated constantly for a continuous supply

from the water companies so as to eliminate the pernicious practice of water storage in filthy butts and cisterns, slimy with algae and fungi and open to all the germs of the atmosphere. And he took every opportunity of publicising the vital importance of the matter by reading papers at scientific meetings and submitting his Annual Reports to the medical journals for review. In February, 1858, he gave a long talk to the Royal Institution (Chapter 11) on "The drinking water of the metropolis", discussing first its chemistry, and the source and implications of some of the chemicals found in impure waters; then the dead and living plant and animal material which could only be demonstrated by microscopical examination of the samples; and finally, methods of purifying water, which he demonstrated by filtering it through charcoal, sand and other substances, especially advocating the use of "iron" for precipitating organic matter.[8]

As well as agitating about water, Lankester was, as we shall see later (Chapter 11), greatly preoccupied with food, its composition, nutrient value and purity. So that when, in 1860, the Act for Preventing the Adulteration of Food and Drink came into force he promptly drew his Vestry's attention to it. The Vestry responded by appointing him Analyst, unpaid; on which he commented that he did not accept the post because it was "necessarily attached to the position of Medical Officer of Health", but only because his experience happened to be peculiarly suited to it. He also pointed out that he would need an office and apparatus, but these were not forthcoming, with the result that in 1862 he reported tartly that he had been carrying out some analyses using his own microscope and "I have been enabled to make use [of apparatus], through the kindness of friends in those parishes where the office of Food Analyst is not a dead letter": and the following year, "I have little or nothing to report with regard to the ... adulteration of food, as the apparatus which you have determined to erect is not yet in a sufficiently advanced state to be practically employed". It was not until 1867, five years after the building of the new, three-storey Vestry Hall that he was finally given an upper room there, and promptly set about analysing the parish water sources. But as for food, "As this office was conferred upon me without any arrangements as to the nature of the duties I was to perform, or the means of performing them, I have little to report on the subject". However, he had analysed a great many milks, and whereas some were good, "many are so entirely deficient in the dietetical constituents of this food, that those who use it are not only cheated out of their money but their food". At some time, perhaps after he had been given the room in the Vestry Hall, the Vestry began to pay him a salary as Analyst, for at his death he was receiving £50 a year for the job.

At this date it was common for even the most reputable of medical men to endorse in print patent medicines which they considered to be particularly valuable to their patients, and inevitably the proprietors of the medicines used the practitioners' names in fulsome advertisements for their wares. The practice was, of course, wide open to abuse, but nevertheless, Lankester occasionally indulged in it, using his official title of Medical Officer of Health. For instance, in a promotional book, *Disinfection and Hygiene* (1860), H.B.Condy, the maker of Condy's Fluid, quoted adulatory letters from a number of doctors, including one from Lankester, praising the product for its excellence in the removal of odours and "arrest of the putrifactive processes". A year later a Leader appeared in the *BMJ* headed "Professional testimonial mongers", in which the writer whoeheartedly condemned the practice, specifically mentioning Lankester, among others, by name. Lankester's sin on this occasion had been his endorsement of Dr. de Jongh's Cod-liver Oil, which had resulted in an advertisement by the makers stating that its "immeasurable therapeutic superiority" had been "incontestably established by the recorded opinions of the most distinguished physicians and surgeons in all parts of the world". The following week the *BMJ* printed a furious reply from Lankester, who considered it his duty as a food analyst to endorse the good. In his opinion it was impossible to distinguish between cod-liver oil as a food and as a medicine (he found it equally difficult to distinguish between the functions of alcohol, when properly used, as a food and a medicine, a problem which got him into trouble with the same Journal at about the same time (Chapter 11)). He then rebutted the imputation that he obtained any financial reward, and suggested that the *Journal*'s eulogies of "trashy" books and of other medical products were equally reprehensible, ending by leaving it open to question as to whether the endorsement system should not be completely abolished.[9,10]

According to Lankester's figures for 1856, the cause of the highest mortality in the parish was "inflammatory diseases of the lungs" (excluding phthisis), which accounted for 138 of the total of 682 deaths. Presumably these diseases were bronchitis and pneumonia, but they are very rarely mentioned in subsequent reports. Only in 1864, when the total number of deaths, at 832, was the highest for nine years, did he point out that all the excess deaths occurred in the exceptionally cold first quarter of the year, that they were evenly spread across the parish, and that they were due to bronchitis. That this group of diseases was the only one for which he never discussed preventive measures suggests that it was regarded as the inevitable result of the British climate, about which nothing could be done.

The next most lethal disease, phthsis, accounted for 110 deaths in 1856. Here Lankester was in no doubt that lack of ventilation was, with overcrowding, one of the main causes, and he returned to the subject again and again. He felt strongly that the problem was exacerbated by the excessive amount of oxygen extracted by the newly introduced gas lighting from the air of already ill-ventilated rooms, together with the carbon dioxide produced. He pointed out that in better-off homes, at least, the evil was often self-inflicted, for there was a general terror of fresh air among rich and poor alike; windows, even if they would open, were kept tightly shut, and ventilators were deliberately blocked. Very early on, as in the case of the Burlington Arcade, he was advocating better ventilation of workshops and factories and a reduction in working hours for young people, together with the provision of parks and open spaces where games could be played and healthy refreshments sold.

Apart from domestic service, one of the more important sources of employment for women and girls was the dress-making trade, where seamstresses worked for long hours in crowded and often ill-ventilated rooms (Fig. 34) and were housed by their employers in even more densely packed dormitories or attics, often sleeping two to a bed. The incidence of consumption among these girls was high, and Lankester made a point of frequent inspection of such premises after one girl died of the disease, combined with overwork.[11] This particular case led him into an angry correspondence with *The Times*, for when that paper reported it, and not unnaturally used his figures for the cubic feet of space per worker in the work-room, he had to write and admit that they were incorrect due to an error on the part of a clerk. *The Times* retorted that the MOH should be responsible for his own clerking, to which Lankester rejoined angrily that he had more important things to do.

The third deadly group of diseases was the so-called "zymotics", which together accounted for 85 deaths in 1856. Lankester considered that all these diseases were largely preventable if proper precautions such as personal cleanliness and the isolation of sick persons were strictly adhered to, though smallpox, he constantly reiterated, could be completely eradicated. To this end he went to extraordinary lengths to seek out and vaccinate every child in the parish, and though he never quite succeeded, the death rate in St. James's, Westminster, in the 1871 epidemic compared very favourably with that of the rest of the metropolis. An Act permitting vaccination had been passed as early as 1840, and in 1853, following a study by the Epidemiological Society, it was made compulsory, but that Act was never fully implemented. It was not until 1871, the year of the London outbreak, that a third Act compelled the local health boards to appoint vaccination officers, and fined parents who refused to have their children vaccinated.

Fig. 34. Exhausted seamstresses at a West End dress-maker's at midnight.

Fig. 35. The public vaccinator.

Lankester had blamed the 1859 outbreak squarely on the fact that "the countrymen of Jenner had neglected the great discovery which he had bequeathed". In that outbreak he called in the existing public vaccinators (Fig. 35) and distributed tracts and leaflets he had composed himself (Fig. 36), but still not every child was reached, one reason, he felt, being that doctors were not prepared to cooperate for the small sum per child which they were paid. He suggested that schools and lodging-houses should be made to check on their pupils and inmates, and employers on their workers; but in 1860 he lost patience and directed his Sanitary Inspector to devote all his time to the job. Morgan visited 1,469 homes and saw 1,919 children at school, finding 448 unvaccinated children in all. Following this effort, Lankester made detailed suggestions to the Vestry for enforcing vaccination, but because the death rate was now so low, nothing was done. It was in vain that he pointed out that it was impossible to isolate St. James's from the surrounding parishes and that unless further action was taken there would be a disaster. "It really is no use to say", he berated his hearers, "it could not be helped and everything had been done to prevent it. If proper precautions had been taken, it could have been helped, and the very things that would have prevented it were not done".[11] In the 1871 outbreak he reported that, as a further precaution, "a capacious and complete disinfecting apparatus having been erected", all clothing and bedding could now be rendered safe and, as usual, he distributed leaflets advising on the precautions to be taken. For further publicity, he wrote an article in *Nature*, "The smallpox epidemic".[12]

Of the two greatest killers among the other zymotic diseases, scarlet fever and (w)hooping cough, Lankester repeated time and time again that they could only be controlled, scarlet fever particularly, by disinfection and isolation, and most specifically, by keeping affected children away from school. In a handbill he issued in 1874 (which was probably a re-issue of a much earlier one), he suggested that, after isolation of the patient, his body should be rubbed all over with oil, a plan found effective by Dr. Budd "for preventing the poison from the skin being disseminated through the air". Again he wrote to *Nature* drawing attention to the seriousness of the situation. Though the death rate from the disease in London at the time was 190 a week there was, he pointed out, no public outcry as there would have been if it had been due to cholera.

I am convinced that the holocaust of victims that we annually offer to this Moloch ... arises from ignorance, and that a general knowledge alone of the facts above stated can suffice to drive from us this plague, so disgraceful alike to our intelligence and our humanity.[13]

SMALL POX AND ITS PREVENTION.

I.—When this highly-contagious and fatal disease prevails in a District, the Inhabitants should be made aware of the danger to which they are exposed, of the best means of preventing the attack of the disease, and of stopping it where it has already broken out.

II.—In the first place it cannot be too widely known that **VACCINATION** is one of the best means of preventing the attack of Small Pox.

III.—All persons should be re-vaccinated after 12 years of age.

IV.—When Small Pox prevails in a family or neighbourhood, every person should be immediately re-vaccinated under the direction of a legally qualified medical practitioner.

V.—It is required by law that every child be vaccinated within three months after its birth, and any parents or persons having charge of infants, and not having them vaccinated, are liable to prosecution and fines for the offence.

VI.—When it has been ascertained that an individual has got Small Pox, everything should be done to separate the person attacked from those around. Where it is deemed desirable to remove persons thus affected to a Small Pox Hospital, information can be obtained, and the means of conveying patients ascertained by applying to the Sanitary Inspector.

VII.—Where persons are found to be labouring under the disease, a Medical Man should be sent for immediately.

VIII.—The following directions should in all cases be carried into effect :—

The room should be cleared of all needless woollen or other draperies which might possibly serve to harbour the poison. A basin, charged with chloride or carbolate of lime, or some other convenient disinfectant, should be kept constantly on the bed for the patient to spit in. A large vessel, containing water impregnated with chlorides, or with Condy's fluid, should always stand in the room for the reception of all bed and body-linen immediately on its removal from the person of the patient. Pocket-handkerchiefs should not be used, and small pieces of rag employed instead for wiping the mouth and nose. Each piece, after being once used, should be immediately burnt. As of necessity, the hands of nurses become frequently soiled by the secretions, a good supply of towels and two basins—one containing water with Condy's fluid or chlorides, and another plain soap and water, should be always at hand for the immediate removal of the taint. All glasses, cups, or other vessels, used by or about the patient, should be scrupulously cleaned before being used by others. The discharges from the bowels and kidneys should be received on their very issue from the body into vessels charged with disinfectants and immediately conveyed away.

No persons should be allowed to enter the room except those who are attending upon the sick. Persons attending upon the sick should be scrupulous in cleaning their hands and disinfecting their clothes before they go out of the sick room, or communicate with those who have not got the disease.

IX.—When persons have had the Small Pox, whether they get well or die, the room in which they have been ill should be disinfected. The floor should be washed with chloride of lime and water, or carbolic acid and water. The paper should be removed by moistening with carbolic acid and water, or with Condy's fluid and water. The room should then be fumigated by burning sulphur in an iron dish, the fireplace, crevices in windows and doors being closed by putting paper over them. The room should be exposed to the sulphur vapour for five or six hours. Or, the room may be fumigated in the same way with chlorine vapour, which is procured by pouring oil of vitriol on common salt and oxide of manganese.

X.—After the room has been fumigated, it should be lime-whited, and the doors and windows kept open for a week or a fortnight.

EDWIN LANKESTER, M.D.,
Medical Officer of Health, St. James's, Westminster.

Dr. Lankester's *Sanitary Instructions.*—No. 4.

Dr. LANKESTER'S SANITARY INSTRUCTIONS. Each 1d.; per dozen 6d.; per 100 4s.; per 1,000 30s.; for General Distribution. 1. Plain Rules for Management of Infants. 2. Scarlet Fever and the best means of preventing it. 3. Typhoid or Drain Fever and its prevention. 4. Small Pox and its prevention. 5. Cholera and Diarrhœa and their prevention. 6 Measles and its prevention.

London: ROBERT HARDWICKE, 192, PICCADILLY.

Fig. 36. Dr. Lankester's Sanitary Instructions. Small Pox. Published by Robert Hardwicke.

He was, of course, over sanguine, for scarlet fever was not conquered until the discovery of antibiotics, by which time the natural virulence of the causal *Streptococcus* was also declining; but the measures he suggested may well have reduced the number of cases. In his article he gave it as his opinion that doctors failed to give advice on preventive measures because they were not trained in public health, and anyhow, he added cynically, it was not in their interest to do so. Later, in a letter replying to one critical of his scathing remarks on the profession, he only re-emphasized them, adding that he could never be induced "to refrain from speaking the truth of [the doctors] in the interests of the public".[14]

Up to the middle of the nineteenth century doctors had found great difficulty, as the names suggest, in distinguishing between typhus and typhoid fevers. We now know that typhus is caused by organisms of the *Rickettsia* group, obligate parasites living within the host cells. It is a louse-borne disease, transmitted through the creature's faeces, and contracted by healthy persons either when they scratch their louse bites, or by inhaling dust containing still viable organisms. Typhus has no gastric sympoms. Typhoid, on the other hand, is caused by *Salmonella typhae*, a bacterium which can live for considerable periods outside the body, and is passed from host to host by faecal contamination following the unclean handling of food. It is characterised by fever, headaches and ulceration of the intestine. Always in his tables Lankester lumps the two diseases together under one heading, "Typhus", although by 1862 at least, he was well aware of the clinical differences between them. Typhus, he wrote in his Report for that year, was a highly contagious disease of overcrowded populations, "delighting in human dirt", and there was little of it in the parish. Typhoid, on the other hand, was the equivalent of gastric fever; it was less contagious than typhus and originated in decomposing animal and vegetable matter; it visited rich and poor alike. "It needs but a single whiff of the poison to produce the disease in those who are predisposed to its attacks". In fact, Sir William Jenner, who had been a fellow student of Lankester's at University College, had been the first to distinguish between the two diseases on pathological as well as on clinical grounds, and Lankester would almost certainly have known his book, *On the Identity or Non-Identity of Typhoid and Typhus Fevers*, published in 1850. As to the cause of typhoid, when addressing his employers he stuck to the well recognized theory of poisonous miasmata given off by decomposing matter, but his own thinking was, as we shall see (Chapter 10), far more advanced. From a practical point of view, however, he was able to boast proudly in 1869 that since he took office his sanitary measures had reduced the deaths in the parish due to typhus/typhoid to one third, from 22 to 7.

Besides the continuing tale of disease, filth and overcrowing a number of other matters engaged Lankester's attention more briefly over the years. Once he considered the evils of prostitution; several times he put in a plea for the proper registration of deaths, especially of infant deaths, and for more coroner's inquests; in 1869 he urged health education in schools, and wrote a book to be used for the purpose (Chapter 11), and the following year he extended his plea to include women and girls. In 1865 he noted that 12,500 people had been injured in street accidents in London that year and put forward an engaging idea to solve the problem:

> In our crowded thoroughfares bridges for foot passengers might be erected, which would enable them to avoid passing between the vehicles. Such structures should be ornamented. Their base might be connected with public urinals.

And on several occasions he advocated the use of earth closets in houses where there was no running water; a very sanitary practice, he held, for "it was a Divine injunction on the Jew to bury the refuse of his household in the earth".

The last Report which he himself wrote was for 1872-73. It was a short one, with little of his usual detailed analysis, and gives the impression that it was written by an exhausted man. However, he was able to claim that over his period of service the death rate in the parish, adjusted for the workhouse, was slightly down, at 19.6 per thousand, and was significantly better than that for London as a whole, at 21.5 per thousand.

Chapter Ten

Professional Groups

It was Lankester's firm belief that the more publicity he could give his cause, the more chance he had of achieving his ends and, as we have seen, he lost no opportunity of publishing and circulating his Annual Reports and writing articles for the medical and scientific press. In addition, he was a founder member of two new professional societies both of which included publicity among their aims. No sooner had the new metropolitan medical officers of health been appointed in 1856 than four of them (of whom Lankester may have been one), realizing the need for solidarity in the face of parsimonious vestries, banded together to form the Metropolitan Association of Medical Officers of Health. They were soon joined by most of the other London Officers, forming a strong pressure group and a forum for discussion of mutual problems. It was this Association which, in 1875, merged with similar societies which had been springing up all over the country to form the nationwide Society of Medical Officers of Health.[1] Lankester was active in the Metropolitan Association from the beginning. He immediately became Chairman of the Food (Adulteration) Committee, and he was on the General Purposes Committee from 1865 to 1869 and its Chairman in 1867-8; he was one of two Vice-Presidents when John Simon was President in 1857-9.

He used the Association's meetings as a scientific debating ground where he could air new ideas which were unsuitable for inclusion in reports to a lay vestry, and one of his longer contributions in this vein, reproduced very fully in the *BMJ*[2] some months *before* he repeated the traditional view of the subject in his Annual Report, was a paper giving an account of the very latest ideas on "The causation of typhoid fever". Many people, he said, recognizing the constant association of the disease with foul sewers and drains, inferred that:

> night soil had a power of generating organic poison which, entering the blood, produced typhoid fever. On the other hand, Dr. William Budd of Bristol, after a very effective study of several outbreaks of typhoid fever, had come to the conclusion that the discharges from the bowels alone, were the exciting causes of typhoid fever. [3,4] ... He had shown that there was no

more reason to attribute a spontaneous origin to typhoid fever than to smallpox: and taking it for granted that the origin of smallpox was specifically the same under all circumstances, he maintained that the same must be true of typhoid fever.

While still accepting the "malarial" origin of many fevers, Lankester went on to agree that there was not sufficient evidence to support it for typhoid; but, as with cholera, he could not bring himself to reject the old theory in its entirety when the new came along. So he hedged his bets once again, claiming that there was very conclusive evidence:

> that exposure to emanations from decaying night-soil, and the contents of drains and cesspools, did produce a state of the system favourable to the development of typhoid fever, when its poisons got access to such persons.

However, he was also prepared to state unequivocally that, like Budd and Snow (Chap. 6), he now accepted that at least some infectious diseases must be attributed to living organisms:

> It was an interesting question for inquiry, as to whether the germs of typhoid fever could be made to grow or increase upon organic matter, out of the body, in the manner in which germs or spores of the mushroom are made to grow by collections of manure. The discovery was yet to be made of the form which typhoid fever poison assumed.

With his usual thoroughness, he ended his talk by appealing to his listeners to "employ preventative agencies which would cover the issues of both theories" until such time as the actual cause of typhoid was discovered.

The second professional society used by Lankester as a platform for his ideas was the National Association for the Promotion of Social Science, founded in 1857 and often known as the Social Science Association. It was a prestigious body, publishing its own *Transactions*, and it's founders included Edwin Chadwick, John Simon and William Farr among others. It was by no means only concerned with public health, it's five departments comprising Law Amendment, Education, Prevention and Repression of Crime and Social Economy, as well as Public Health; while Lankester was primarily concerned with the last named, he read papers at meetings of the others from time to time. From 1860 to 1872 he held office in one capacity or another in the Public Health Department and on the Executive Committee of the Association's Council, often alongside his old friend and fellow student, Robert Hardwicke, who was now MOH for Paddington. At most of the Association's Annual Meetings Lankester read papers or contributed to discussions on the topics appearing in his current Annual Report. His advanced thinking on public health matters was very much in tune with that of this enterprising Association, which aimed at "reducing the deaths in every employment, in all inhabited localities to the level of those which occur in the healthiest employments and in the healthiest localities".[5] In those days before the widespread adoption of statistics, members worked to encourage their use in health matters, setting out to collect evidence on the existing state of public health and on ways of improving it.

Among Lankester's major contributions to meetings was a paper in 1860, suggested to him by Edwin Chadwick, giving an account of the results of sanitary legislation in London, to which end he reported at length on the problems and actions of a MOH as exemplified by his own parish. In 1864 he spoke on sewage and the problem of its disposal without gross pollution of the rivers; and the same year he made long contributions both on the registration of births and deaths, and on overcrowding. In 1867 it was the turn of the nutritional content of foods, and more particularly, of prison and workhouse dietaries, which he regarded as inexcusably inadequate. Two years later the meeting was held in Bristol, William Budd's home city, where Lankester shared the Vice-Presidency with Budd and read a paper on one of his great enthusiasms, "The teaching of physiology as a branch of general education".

The Association's *Transactions*, published annually, contained detailed reports of meetings, but it was felt that there was a need for the publication of other relevant papers as well. This seems to have been the origin of the short-lived *Journal of Social Science*, the two volumes of which appeared in 1865 and 1866, edited by Lankester. In the first volume, in a report of the Ninth Annual Meeting of the Association, an account is given of a paper on an outbreak of cattle plague (rinderpest), during the discussion of which two contributors gave it as their opinion that the disease, which the speaker had shown to have been imported from abroad, was in fact the result of the filthy conditions in which cows were kept in towns in this country. Taking full advantage of his position as Editor, Lankester devoted the next page and a half to his own most vehement reply.

He said he stood there to denounce most thoroughly and determinately all attempts to persuade the people of this country that contagious diseases were not contagious. Nothing could be so frightfully dangerous, especially at the present time, as an attempt to divert the attention of the people from the resisting of contagious poison, and to convince them that it was in their own houses and homes that the disease was to be engendered.

He was again using the word "contagious" as we would use "infectious" today. He went on to emphasize that the speaker had shown beyond doubt that rinderpest had been imported, and to give specific examples, known to him personally, of how, once in this country, the disease had spread from herd to herd by contact. His unexpected and extremely forceful intervention in a discussion on a veterinary matter was undoubtedly provoked by his concern at the way in which the infectious nature of diseases such as scarlet fever was being played down at the time.[6]

Also in the first volume of the *Journal* is a two-part article from his own pen, "Notes for a history of sanitary legislation", which covered the sanitary laws of the Romans, Jews and Moslems from the earliest times, modern European legislation, and ended up with a detailed review of recent British Acts of Parliament.* His final comment was:

> What is really wanted in our country is an intelligent community to take an interest in matters relating to public health. Our present sanitary defects are all more or less traceable to the culpable practice of omitting from our system of education an inculcation of a knowledge of those laws by which God governs the life and health of man. These laws have been ignored and trodden underfoot alike by the so-called educated and refined as by the ignorant masses, and the consequences have been the dire judgements of the Almighty in the form of poverty, pestilence and death.

We shall see (Chap. 11) the tremendous efforts he was making at the time to promote his ideal of an education in biology for all.

---

* This article also formed the first part of an entry for "Hygiene" written by Lankester for the Eighth Edition of the *Encyclopaedia Brittanica* in about 1860. Its title implies that its author had intended to expand it to book form, but the *British Library Catalogue* includes no reference to any book of a similar title. In 1867, however, the *MTG*[7] reviewed a 35-page booklet by Lankester, under the same title, published by Chapman and Hall. It seems likely that the "Notes" were eventually printed as they stood rather than expanded.

Chapter Eleven

South Kensington   1857-1864

Repeatedly over the years Lankester had, as we have seen, emphasized and re-emphasized the importance, for their own health and happiness, of a public with at least a basic knowledge of physiology and nutrition; and by "the public" he meant *all* the public - the poor as well as the rich, and women and children as well as men. Long before his appointment as MOH he had lectured and written to this end to both professional and lay people, for instance in his Introductory Lecture at New College in 1851:

> A knowledge of the fundamental facts of physiology appear to me to be the most necessary of human requirements ... There can be no well-being to the human body unless it be subject to the conditions of natural existence. These conditions must be understood, not alone by the rulers of the country, but by every individual.

After 1856 he redoubled his efforts, his last popular book appearing in the year of his death. He started with his fellow professionals by translating from the German for them, in 1857, F. Kuechenmeister's *On Animal and Vegetable Parasites of the Human Body*. This was of great importance to contemporary British dermatology, for it stated for the first time in English that ringworm is caused by fungi, and described the appearance of the organisms in lesions. The translation was quickly siezed upon by the brilliant young dermatologist W. Tilbury Fox (another of Hardwicke's authors), who based on it his pioneering *Skin Diseases of Parasitic Origin*.[1]

Lankester's next venture was a series of lectures for the Royal Institution, a body which had been founded in 1799 by a group of wealthy and aristocratic landowners bent on exploiting their estates to the maximum in the context of the agrarian revolution then taking place. Such exploitation would serve the double purpose of providing better conditions and more food for the starving and riotous peasantry, and more wealth for the landowners. To this end the Institution had, within a few years of its founding, recruited the most eminent scientists to its ranks and built its own lecture theatre and laboratory. In the latter Sir

Humphrey Davy carried out soil analyses for the landowners, assessed the nutritive value of grasses, and studied the turnip fly and the means of controlling it; while in the theatre "fashionable" lectures were given in the afternoons, and serious, scientific lectures in the evenings. By the middle of the nineteenth century, however, the place of the Royal Institution in education and science had been usurped by new establishments such as London University, the Royal College of Chemistry and the Royal School of Mines, and the Institute had become more and more of an amateur body.[2] This was its status when Lankester gave his first lecture there in February, 1858, on his favourite topic, "The drinking water of the metropolis" (Chap. 9), followed by a series of five more, given between April and July, on "The vegetable kingdom in relation to the life of man".[3,4] Nevertheless, the lectures were detailed and scientific and included tables classifying the essential ingredients of food and water, and the mineral contents of various foods, a matter with which he was greatly concerned. He discussed the relationships between minerals and human life (though of course he knew nothing of the trace elements) and went into considerable detail about the use of phosphates in agriculture; other lectures concerned lime and "carbonaceous matter" in agriculture, and sugars, oils and fats in nutrition.

There was at the time much discussion about the health-giving properties of ozone, an idea which Lankester strongly supported though others were less convinced. He had invented an "ozonometer" to measure the gas, and took advantage of the meeting of the British Association at Leeds that year to exhibit the instrument for the first time.[5] It consisted of a moving strip of paper impregnated with potassium iodide and starch, attached to a time-clock. When the potassium iodide was oxidised by the ozone the liberated iodine reacted with the starch to give a blue colour, the intensity of which was measured over 24 hours. By means of this machine Lankester had calculated that the amount of ozone in London's atmosphere was nil, compared with 22 units at Blackheath and 55 at Felixstowe. He exhibited the machine again at a meeting of the Metropolitan Association of Medical Officers of Health in 1859, but doubters there reported that other gases could induce the same reaction.[6] Undaunted, he showed it for the third time at the International Exhibition of 1862 in Class XIII, "Philosophical Instruments and Processes depending on their Use" (p. 129). No comment from the jurors is recorded.[7]

It was at about this time that the opportunity arose for Lankester to promote in a new way his great project of health education for all, an opportunity which, despite the onerous nature of his existing commitments, he could in no way resist. The Society of Arts (now the Royal Society of Arts) is, in fact, an abbreviation of the much more accurate, Society for the Encouragement of Arts, Manufactures and

Commerce, which had been founded in the mid-eighteenth century. Its functions had changed over the years until, by the 1850s, paper-reading meetings on matters of current concern, and in-depth enquiries stimulated by them, had become the Society's most important activities; from 1852, these were recorded in its *Journal*.

Among its interests was research into money-saving inventions, such as cheap heating systems, which could improve the living conditions of the poor, and it also helped to establish local museums for the education of the working classes. It was a prestigious society of which many well-known people such as Edwin Chadwick and Karl Marx were members. The date at which Lankester joined is uncertain, but he was a well established member in 1860, for in April of that year he was chairing a meeting at which he also read a paper on a new process for the large scale manufacture of bread. There was considerable disquiet at the time at the routine use of alum in bread-making, for the dual purpose of controlling the yeast fermentation and whitening the product. The new process suggested the replacement of yeast, and hence also of alum, by a solution of carbon dioxide under pressure; when the pressure was suddenly released, the bread would rise.

A few years before this the Society, in its educational capacity, had put on display small exhibitions of food and of animal products, and in 1858 these were presented to the newly erected South Kensington Museum, one of the by-products of the Great Exhibition of 1851. In 1853 the Commissioners for that Exhibition, prompted by Prince Albert, had proposed that the profits should be devoted to popular education in science and the arts, and to this end they had purchased a site in South Kensington for development as a centre for the great project. The Department of Science and Art (usually known as "South Kensington" because its headquarters were on the site) was set up as a subsidiary to the Education Department to administer the project. One of the earliest buildings to be erected was the South Kensington Museum, a temporary, corrugated iron structure which soon attracted the name "Brompton Boilers" (Figs 37,38), because it stood near the old Brompton Road on the part of the site now occupied by the Victoria and Albert Museum.[8,9] The majority of the exhibits were artistic in nature, but there was also a small science collection which included food and animal products[10], mainly those from the Society of Arts.[11]

Supposing that Lankester had been a member of the Society in 1858, he would have been well-known to the members responsible for transferring the collections to the South Kensington Museum. In any case, he must have known Lyon Playfair who was a fellow member of the Social Science

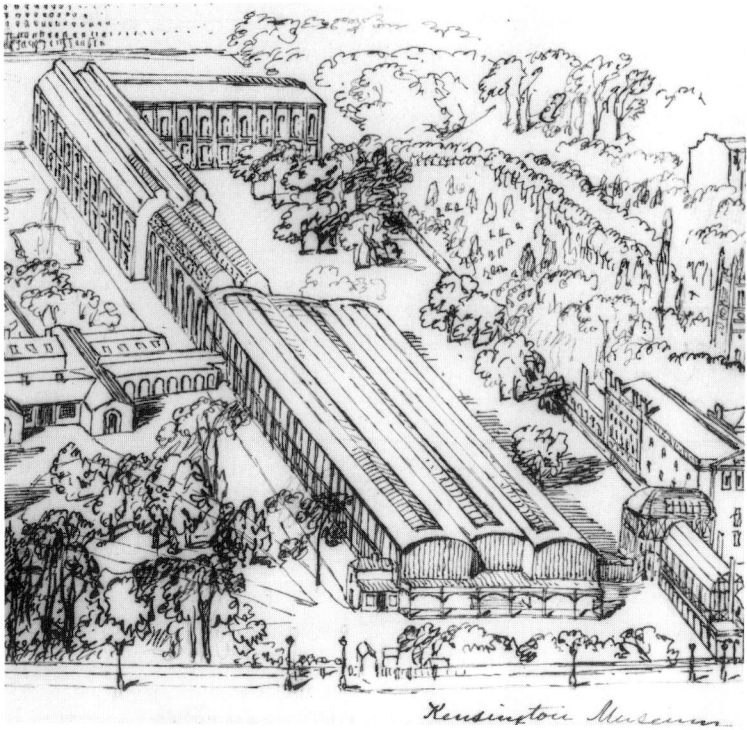

Kensington Museum

Fig. 37. The South Kensington Museum, known as the "Brompton Boilers".

Fig. 38. The entrance to "The Boilers".

Society and had now become Secretary for Science at the Department of Science and Art. It was probably through one or both of these connections that, on 14 October, 1858, Lankester succeeded Playfair (who was taking up the post of Professor of Chemistry at Edinburgh) as part-time Superintendent of the Food and Animal Products collections at South Kensington, and set about using every opportunity the position offered of spreading his gospel of health education to all classes of society.

The appointment was for six months in the first place, for which he would be paid £150 for two days' work per week, his duties, according to the Manuscript Minutes of the Department, to include:

1) General superintendence of the two collections, responsibility for their arrangement, classification, labelling etc.

2) To revise and superintend new additions to the catalogue of the Animal Products Museum, and to prepare, with the assistance of Mr. Thompson [the Keeper] a catalogue of the Food Museum.

3) Generally to perform the duties discharged by Dr. Playfair.

In practice, Lankester seems to have left most of the responsibility for the Animal Products collection to Mr. Thompson while he himself concentrated on Food. Annual Reports were made to the Department in all of which Lankester's constant complaint was of lack of space. He was forced, he reported to display specimens in bottles rather than on trays, though "display on a flat surface is superior educationally", and specimens should be well spaced out so that "the attention may be wholly given to the object looked at without interference of surrounding objects". The intention of the collection, he noted, was to show the composition of foods, so that tables of analyses both by himself and by well known chemists were included. Perishable foods such as fruit and fungi were shown as models, and animals and fish were stuffed.

The catalogue suggested in his original brief was replaced in 1859 by a 96-page *Guide to the Food Collection at South Kensington*, which included not only foods, but stimulants and narcotics as well. But first came an analysis of the chemical composition of the body tissues, including some ideas strange to us today. Among the "Ultimate Elements" was silicon, "which enters into the composition of the teeth and bones": and the "Proximate Principles", the combinations of the "Ultimate Elements", included "gelatin, of which the walls of cells and many tissues of the body, as the skin and hairs, are principally composed". There was, as might be expected of Lankester, a large display on Water, using the various water sources of St. James's, Westminster, including the Broad Street pump, as examples; and a special display of adulterations of foodstuffs, based on the work of Dr. Hassell. The latter showed how tea might be contaminated with black lead or with copper or lead carbonate, cocoa with brick dust, sugar with marble, and that there was water "in almost everything" (Fig. 39). The public was given the opportunity of examining contaminated food through a microscope. A second edition of the *Guide* in 1860 reported a considerable expansion of the collection, and evening as well as daytime opening had been instituted every weekday.

In June, 1859, Lankester took up a further appointment with the Department of Science and Art. It was announced that the first public examination for serving school-teachers would be held in November under its auspices, in a wide variety of subjects. There were no text-books or special courses to prepare the candidates; any teacher who felt he had a chance could sit the examination in the subject(s) of his choice. Lankester and T. H. Huxley were appointed as examiners in Botany and Zoology at a rate of 15 guineas for up to 20 candidates, 5 guineas being allowed for personal attendance and preparation of the syllabus, 5 guineas for preparation of the papers, and 5 guineas for marking them. Great care was taken by the Department over the marking because, as one of the officials put it:

> Teachers whose pay depends entirely on examination have the right to expect that it shall be well done ... the men who set and mark the papers have to be the best available ... especially in the view of the laborious and repulsive nature of the work. Men among the most eminent should hold such posts. [11]

At the first examiners' meeting, held shortly before the examinations, marking was standardised and it was decided that 20% of the papers would be remarked. (Lankester had had previous experience in marking public examinations, for in June 1856, he had been appointed as one of the Examiners in Natural Science for the Civil Service of the East India Company[12]). There were only two candidates in Botany in that first year; one failed, and the other, Mordecai Cubitt Cooke, the 34-year old teacher at a slum school in Lambeth, obtained a first class pass. His path was destined to cross with Lankester's again on several future occasions.

At the Museum Lankester was finding that his appointment for two days a week allowed insufficient time for the work which he considered necessary, and in June, 1860, he wrote to the Department proposing that it should be extended to three days to allow for the preparation of a third edition of the *Guide,* for which he requested payment at 3 guineas per sheet for revised work and 10 guineas for new. The Department agreed to the extra day's work, but cut down heavily on the remuneration, despite which the third and much enlarged edition of the *Guide* appeared later in

THE USE OF ADULTERATION.

Little Girl. "IF YOU PLEASE, SIR, MOTHER SAYS, WILL YOU LET HER HAVE A QUARTER OF A POUND OF YOUR BEST TEA TO KILL THE RATS WITH, AND A OUNCE OF CHOCOLATE AS WOULD GET RID OF THE BLACK BEADLES?"

Fig. 39. The adulteration of food. *Punch,* 4 August, 1855.

the year. Fungi were now included and there was much more detail in all sections, mere lists being replaced by descriptions.

Lankester's enthusiasm for his job was, as usual, unbounded, and in August he proposed a new departure - that he should deliver a series of public lectures on the collections at the Museum on Tuesday evenings. He was granted the use of the theatre at £1 per night, but it was specifically stated that "the priviledge was not to be considered a precedent". Nevertheless, the lectures were repeated in 1861, when 1/- per head was charged for a series of six lectures on food, and an average of 284 persons attended each lecture. A further six lectures on animal products attracted an audience of 170 per lecture, but a course on Saturday afternoons in the summer produced, understandably, an average attendance of only 55 persons. On top of all this, he and T. H. Huxley also started courses at the Royal School of Mines in Jermyn Street for teachers sitting for the Department's examinations.

With his friend Robert Hardwicke, Lankester published his Museum lectures in two books; *The Uses of Animals in Relation to Man* (1860), and *On Food. Being a Course of Lectures Delivered at the South Kensington Museum* (1861). Both are divided into two courses, and the Introductions are revealing. The first course, Lankester wrote, was actually given, and was published in the conversational style in which it was delivered. The second course was written from notes because "it was considered that my public instruction at the Museum should be discontinued": the Department had begun to clamp down on its over enthusiastic employee. *The Uses of Animals* included silk, wool, leather, bone, soap, waste, sponges and corals, shell-fish, insects, furs and feathers, and animal perfumes; while Food covered everything in the Collection and much more. Both books were illustrated with wood engravings (Fig. 40 a,b). Both the medical and lay presses were loud in their praise for the books; for instance, of *On Food* the *Lancet* wrote:

> Full of sound science, curious anecdotes and quaint illustrations, Dr. Lankester has a singular power of illustrative keenness, an overflowing wealth of minute collateral information, which is always brought to the level of the last achievement of science. [13]

Of the chapter on Waste in *The Uses of Animals*, the *Athenaeum* commented:

> Dr. Lankester finds a use for everything, and he delights in analysing each fresh sample of rejected material, and stating how each of its component parts can be turned to best account.[14]

Fig. 1.

ON OIL, BUTTER, AND FAT.

IN this Lecture I shall continue to draw your attention to that class of foods which we know by the name of heat-giving.

This group may very well be divided into—first, those which contain starch and sugar, of which I have already spoken; and, secondly, those which contain oil or fat.

There is a great difference in the chemical composition of oils and fats, as compared with starch and sugar, which can be easily made apparent.

Taking, then, the composition of starch and sugar as carbon 12, hydrogen 10, and oxygen 10, which would express generally the composition of starch and sugar; or, taking the real weights, carbon 72, hydrogen 10, and oxygen 80, the quantity of carbon in

ON WATER.

THE object I have in view in this course of Lectures is to bring under notice the principal forms of those subtances of which we partake, from day to day, under the name of Food; by means of which we live, and without which we should die. The life of man is like a fire. Just as the fire must have fuel in order that it may burn, so we must have food in order that we may live; and the analogy is in many respects quite correct; for we find that man really produces in his body a certain amount of heat, just as the fire does, and the result of the combustion of the materials of his food is the same as the result of burning fuel in a fire. Man, in fact, exists in consequence of the physical and chemical changes that go on in his body as the result

Fig. 40 a, b. Chapter headings from *On Food* (1861).

The books are indeed a delight to read.

Lankester's opinions on alcohol, as propounded in *On Food*, led to two leaders and a brisk correspondence in the *British Medical Journal*. While admitting its pleasurable qualities he regarded it, when used in moderation, as a medicine or auxilliary food:

> It is one of those creatures of a kind Providence by the abuse of which we bring down upon ourselves an everlasting curse, and by the right use of which our highest and best feelings may be kindled towards the Maker and Giver of all good.

The leader writer, who obviously had strong teetotal tendencies, chided Lankester for sitting on the fence, urging him to admit the unmitigated evil of alcohol, but Lankester, Non-Conformist though he was, would have nothing to do with so puritanical a view, and the ensuing correspondence represented all shades of opinion.[15]

By November, 1860, a tone of carping criticism of the Superintendent of the Collections was creeping into the Departmental Minutes:

> My Lords wish him to confine his attention solely to explanatory labels until these are completed; special attention to be given to unlabelled exhibits rather than to revising Dr. Playfair's labels. They do not wish Dr. Lankester to concern himself with the actual work of arrangement, which they consider to be the duty of the Keeper [of Animal Products]. They consider it is not desirable to revise the Catalogue extensively: descriptions of undescribed subjects should be introduced as copies of the labels.

The Department was clearly determined to live up to a recent report on the Museum by an investigating committee which had been greatly impressed by the cost-effectiveness of the institution,[11] and was warning its Superintendent to confine himself to the niggling routine jobs which had been specified in his original brief and to waste no further time on the broader issues which were, strictly speaking, outside it. Despite this he tried, a few months later, to persuade the Department to buy a foreign collection of animal products which he felt would broaden the scope of the Museum, and in July, 1861, he received from M. C. Cooke (who had done so well in Botany in the first Teachers' Examination) a collection of seaweeds, mosses, lichens and their products, having exchanged them for other specimens in the Museum so that no costs were incurred.

On 24 July, 1862, the Department finally lost patience with its Superintendent and the axe fell. The Minute for that date reads:

The arrangement for the duties hitherto performed by Dr. Lankester will in future be in accordance with the Minute relating to scientific services.

The next page of the Minute Book is missing. Four days later Lankester claimed payment for both the new and revisional work he had carried out on the *Guides*, but the Department would only pay him for the new, adding:

His services are not required further being unsatisfactory and hardly justifying the amount recommended by the Chief Clerk. To this amount My Lords adhere.

The argument about his position, and in particular about his Annual Report for 1862, continued into 1863, the Department pointing out that the appointment had always been a temporary one subject to six-monthly renewal, and refusing to reconsider this. As regards the Annual Report:

My Lords consider that Dr. Lankester's Annual Report directly relates to work not coming within his province as Scientific Superintendent, and that it fails to convey an accurate idea of the amount of scientific work performed by him ... My Lords direct that Dr. Lankester be requested to furnish another report which shall set forth specifically and be limited to his scientific work only.

The argument about payment for the *Guides* rumbled on, but the Department could not be persuaded to give him more than £55.14.0, though he claimed £132. An exasperated Minute on 1 July stated baldly that Lankester was to be informed that:

My Lords will not require his services in future in connection with the Food and Animal Museums.

In August, after a further letter from Lankester, My Lords insisted that "there was no question of arbitration", and that "his services are terminated in respect of the Food Museum for the same reason as the Animal Museum, because they were unsatisfactory". When Lankester still persisted, the consequent Minute in October reads simply:

Read Dr. Lankester's letter of 13 August. My Lords decline to continue the correspondence.

Thus, with the inevitable clash between an employer bent on sticking to the letter of the law in order to keep expenses to a minimum, and an idealistic employee with thoughts only for the public good, ended Lankester's connection with the South Kensington Museum. Writing in *Nature* years later, *á propos* of a series of lectures on food for which an entry fee was being charged which was beyond the means of the poor, he commented bitterly of the provision of cheap lectures that:

> It cannot be done at South Kensington; the experiment has been tried there and failed. The country gentlemen in the House of Commons do not see their way to voting public money for the instruction of the people of London. [16]

Lankester's entry in the *Dictionary of National Biography* implies that his employment at South Kensington was terminated because he had obtained the post of Coroner for Central Middlesex (Chap. 12), but the Department's Minutes make it absolutely clear that, as far as it was concerned, the sole reason for his dismissal was the unsatisfactory nature of his work - his refusal to confine himself to its narrow interpretation of the job. Despite all his considerable powers of persuasion, he was quite unable to move his employers one step beyond their Civil Service brief. However, it is indeed difficult to see how he could both have retained this post and carried out the duties of a coroner, while still remaining Medical Officer of Health for St. James's, Westminster, a position which he appeared to have no intention of relinquishing.

The termination of his appointment as Examiner for the Teacher's Examinations was as abrupt as that to the Museum. A letter from him to the Secretary, pasted into the Minute Book on 22 October, 1864, is written in large, scrawled handwriting which could imply either that he was ill or very angry:

> I beg to acknowledge the receipt of your letter of the 17th inst, and to express my surprise that My Lords should have requested another person to make the examinations in Botany rather than myself. I was not prepared for this, and so late as the 29th June last My Lords requested me to run up a short general report upon the actions of the Science Minute on the scientific instruction of the industrious classes. I must now beg of you to enquire of My Lords if they wish me to answer that letter, and also why they have withdrawn from me an appointment which I have done the best to discharge in an honorable and efficient manner.

Their Lordships must have had considerable difficulty in replying to this for their draft letter, attached to the Minutes, is heavily scored out and overwritten. However, they did not feel called upon to give reasons for the dismissal, as the appointment had never been a permanent one; and as to the report, all the other examiners had already handed theirs in and his was not now required. This was not the first occasion on which Lankester's dilatoriness in replying to correspondence had got him into difficulties, and it would not be the last, but one cannot escape the conclusion that in this case it was used as a convenient excuse by the Department for finally ridding themselves of an employee who they regarded as thoroughly troublesome.

Lankester's one remaining scientific commitment at South Kensington was with the 1862 International Exhibition which was to be held there, and for which he had been appointed President of Section B (Preparations of Food used for Human Consumption) in· Class B (Substances used as Food). He had 12 jurors under him, including J. D. Hooker of Kew. His own exhibit, the ozonmeter, appeared in another Section.

While he was working for the Department of Science and Art he had not been idle in other fields of popular science. He had been joint editor of the *Quarterly Journal of Microscopical Science* for six years when, in 1859, he was elected President of the Microscopical Society of London, an honour to be followed by a second term in 1860. His Presidential Address the first year started with a résumé of the history of the microscope and of recent advances in its construction. Then, going on to show how recent major scientific discoveries such as the cell theory had been made by men with very wide interests, he condemned narrow specialization and urged each member of the Society to take an interest in all aspects of microscopy, at least by attending talks and joining in discussions on subjects other than their own. He also complained that, though the British had played a major part in the development and perfection of the microscope, its practical use had, until very recently, been largely ignored by the professions and learned societies, and left to members of their own Society. In his Address the following year he was able to note that the reverse trend had begun, and the Microscopical Society was losing members to the learned societies.[17,18]

Perhaps it was to coincide with his term as President that Lankester brought out, in 1859, what was to become his immensely popular *Half Hours with the Microscope*, published by Robert Hardwicke. The price of basic microscopes at this period was not unreasonable, and microscopy was becoming a favourite pastime for amateurs, a trend which Lankester, of all people, would be keen to encourage. In his first chapter he wrote:

What eyes would be to the man who is born blind, the Microscope is to the man who sees only with his naked eye. It opens a new world to him, and thousands of objects whose form and shape, and even existence, he could only imagine, can now be observed with accuracy.

Over one quarter of the little 106-page book is devoted to the structure and use of the instrument and its accessories, including the camera lucida, and an appendix gives instruction on the preparation and mounting of objects. In between are chapters on 250 objects which can be found and examined in the countryside, the garden, the pond, the seaside and indoors, all beautifully illustrated from life (Fig. 41) and described in the flowing text, for instance:

> The red appearance on the leaves of wheat, called the rust, is due to one of these fungi ... This [referring to the figure] appears to be an early stage of the fungus, which produces what is called mildew, ... These fungi are so common on the wheat-plant that their spores mingle with the seeds when ground into flour, and can be found, when carefully sought for, in almost every piece of bread that is examined under the microscope.*

By 1863 over 7,000 copies of the book had been sold, and the fifth and last edition appeared as late as 1905.

For some years past Lankester had been extending the frontiers of health education by lecturing on physiology at what must have been a very advanced girls' school.[19] Now he widened his audience further by speaking to the Ladies' Sanitary Association on *Sanitary Defects and Medical Shortcomings* (1859) and publishing his talk as a 32-page booklet. The members of this Association were middle class women whose original purpose had been to overcome the ignorance of science and sanitation imposed on them by the social mores of the age, so that they could not only improve the health and hygiene of their own families, but help the less fortunate to better their lot as well. It had tended, however, to become a society of do-gooders, and Lankester set out to change its direction. The title of the talk was not of the speaker's own choosing and, as he pointed out, it was a very wide one, and the lecture must have been very long. It was also very courageous of him, as a medical man himself, and one who had already fallen foul of a Royal College, to be prepared to criticize his own profession to a lay audience.

His own parish of St. James's, Westminster, would, he thought, provide excellent examples of the problems of rich and poor alike. As reading matter, he particularly recommended to his audience Florence Nightingale's recent book, *Notes on Nursing*, about which:

> you would think it the trained intellect of the physiologist that had got into this tender, delicate female frame - there is so much knowledge and decision combined with its love and tenderness.

---

* See Chapter 6 and the cholera fungus controversy.

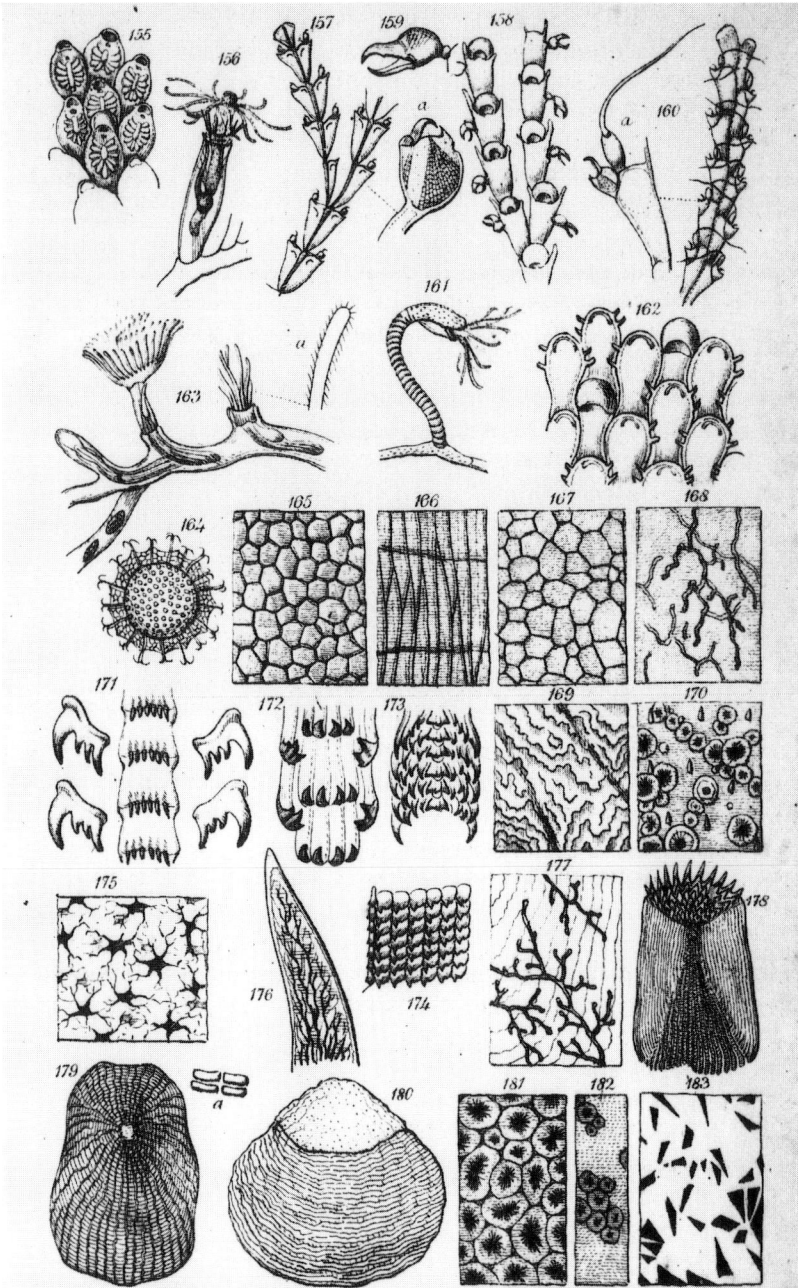

Fig. 41. Illustration from *Half Hours with the Microscope* (1859) showing objects to be found at the seaside.

Then came the first brave criticism of his own profession:

Many medical men condemn this book on account of what they call its "rash assertions"; but recollect, with regard to medical men, that they have not fully entered into this subject. They have rather studied physiology in relation to the cure of disease, than in its relations to the preservation of health.

The talk was a practical one, for having pointed out that unless the housewife kept an eye on her own sinks and drains, no-one else was likely to do so, he put on a display of sink traps and their workings, and then showed his audience how to test for organic impurities in water with potassium permanganate. On several occasions during the talk he attempted to change the ladies' approach to their poorer sisters when they were out on their errands of mercy:

You must not go and talk about their [the poor] being dirty people. What you ought to do is to influence the authorities, and get water supplied to the top of the house.

And they should report insanitary conditions to the MOH, because it was the duty of the landlord to rectify them. His whole attitude to health is summed up in his last paragraph:

I don't know whether, as a medical man, I ought to say this, lest my professional brethren should consider I am depreciating them in any way [but] they have all had too much faith in medicine ... I wish to show that it would be perfectly useless to carry on your Association merely as a sentimental body.

It is useless to talk about health if you know nothing about it, he said, but you will really save life if you understand the laws of health yourself:

Now that we do see our way to understanding these great laws of health, the time has come for your Association to act efficiently.

In their private life at this time, the Lankesters had completed their family of seven children by 1860, the youngest, Alfred Owen (who was destined to become what his father never achieved, a consultant physician) having been born the previous year. Phebe, who was still only 35 years old, wasted no time in embarking on a new career, that of botanical authoress, aided and abetted by her husband. The study and collection of wild flowers was an acceptable pursuit for the wives of gentlemen, but Phebe was more than a dilettante; probably with the encouragement of Edwin, she had become an accomplished botanist in her own right. Her publisher, of course, being Robert Hardwicke, her first book, *British Ferns* (1860), appeared in his "Plain and Easy" series. It was fully illustrated in colour and included a botanical classification and details of the structure and function of ferns, as well as instructions for their cultivation. The book appeared at the height of the great Victorian fern craze, when all sections of society were vying with each other in collecting ferns from the wild and cultivating them in gardens, tanks and Wardian cases; but it proved so popular that it far outlived the craze, running to four editions, the last published by W.H. Allen in 1890.

The year after publishing *British Ferns*, Hardwicke produced Phebe's second book, *Wild Flowers Worth Notice for their Beauty, Uses and Associations*, a most delightful small book illustrated in colour by the great botanical artist, J. E. Sowerby. It too was extremely popular and last appeared in Allen's edition of 1890.

M. C. Cooke, meanwhile, who had left teaching shortly after taking the Department's examination in Botany, and was now eking out a living in a variety of part-time jobs, had for some years been an enthusiastic promoter of educational museums. Entirely on his own initiative he had set one up in his own school, Holy Trinity, Lambeth, and he was also a prime mover in starting the Scholastic Museum for the use of all metropolitan school-teachers. At the time of his exchange of specimens with the Food Museum he was not only lecturing in botany to classes of working men, but was engaged in cataloguing Indian and New Zealand exhibits for the International Exhibition of 1862. Between 1858 and 1860 he also wrote a number of articles for the *Journal* of the Society of Arts, though he was never a member of that body. He and Lankester, therefore, had much in common, and the older man had evidently taken Cooke under his wing for in about 1860 he introduced Cooke to Robert Hardwicke at the latter's premises at 192 Piccadilly, thus bringing about the start of a most fruitful partnership and a new career for Cooke. Cooke's first venture, probably encouraged by Lankester, was to publish two small volumes, *The Manual of Structural Botany* (1861) and *The Manual of Botanic Terms* (1862), specifically for candidates for the Teachers' Examination for which, when he sat for it, neither text-books nor lectures were available. Both books were popular and ran to a number of editions.[20]

Robert Hardwicke's personal interest in his author's scientific activities has already been mentioned. Cooke had two great and lifelong enthusiasms, a mission to pass on his own love of Nature to his fellow men, and a fascination with fungi, large and small: he would soon become one of Britain's leading mycologists. In furthering these enthusiasms, as well as Cooke's career, Hardwicke would play a not inconsiderable part. In 1862 he encouraged Cooke to write a book on *British Fungi* for his "Plain and Easy" series. It was not only Cooke's first book on fungi, but the first popular book on the group ever written. In the same year Cooke founded a botanical field club, the Society of Amateur Botanists, which met on Hardwicke's premises and had a brass plate announcing the fact at the entrance to the shop. Both Cooke and Lankester were frequent visitors to the shop, the latter often bringing with him his eldest son, Ray, then aged about 15 and already a keen naturalist. This was doubtless how Ray became one of the first, and certainly the youngest, member of the Society of Amateur Botanists.[21]

At the end of the Society's first year of existence, Cooke delivered his Presidential Address in his usual flamboyant style, ending with a quotation from Wordsworth's "Lines composed a few miles above Tintern Abbey", including the words: "Nature never did betray the heart that loved her", his favourite quotation, which his daughter had engraved on his tombstone. These same lines had been used by Phebe Lankester the previous year in her preface to *Wild Flowers Worth Notice*. Cooke had undoubtedly read the book; was it here that he first read the lines?

Meanwhile, Phebe was building on her success as a botanical writer. Hardwicke had undertaken to republish James Sowerby's marvellous illustrations of British wild flowers in an edition in which J. T. B. Syme would provide the botanical descriptions; but to complement these, Phebe was asked to write the more popular accounts of the flowers. The first volume of this major work appeared in 1863 as *Syme's English Botany*, other parts following for some years thereafter. Between 1861 and 1864 both the Lankesters and Cooke also contributed articles on a variety of subjects to Hardwicke's periodical publication, *The Popular Science Review*. Few publishers could have done more to provide outlets for their authors.

The Society of Amateur Botanists flourished for three years, until Cooke and two friends started another and more ambitious group, the Quekett Microscopical Club, with which the Amateur Botanists could not compete. Cooke emphasized from the first that the Quekett was intended to complement the august Microscopical Society of London, not to undermine it. His intention was to provide informal, less intimidating conditions that did the older Society, in which beginners, guided by a few experts could learn their craft, and to organise field excursions during which they could collect fresh material for study. Once again, Hardwicke offered his premises as headquarters, and he was quickly elected the Club's first Treasurer. But when it was suggested that Cooke should become President he demurred and put forward the name of Edwin Lankester, pointing out that as a past President of the Microscopical Society, and the long-standing editor of the *Quarterly Journal*, the future friendship of the two societies would thus be assured. Between them, Cooke and Hardwicke persuaded the already overworked Lankester to preside over the Quekett for its first year, and the policy paid off handsomely, for many eminent members of the Microscopical Society joined the Quekett as well, enjoying its informal atmosphere and passing on their expertise to the beginners.[22] At the end of his year of office the Committee, in thanking Lankester for his services, noted that he was "ever foremost in any movement having for its object the advancement of Popular Science".[23] He played no active part in the Club's affairs after that year, but the Quekett is still alive and flourishing today.

Chapter Twelve

Coroner for Central Middlesex 1862-1873

On 11 May, 1862, the death was reported of Mr. Thomas Wakley, Member of Parliament for Finchley, Coroner for West Middlesex, and founder and sometime editor of the *Lancet*. He had devoted his whole life to the reform of the medical profession, used his journal to disseminate recent medical discoveries outside the privileged circle of the great London hospitals, and was fearless in exposing nepotism and injustice. As coroner he fought for reforms against huge establishment opposition but with the overwhelming approval of public opinion, but at his death there was still much to be done. As MOH, Lankester too had frequently called for reforms in the coronership (e.g. in his 1859 Annual Report), so that the vacancy in West Middlesex must have been of considerable interest to him.

The office of Coroner is a very ancient one, and its functions and the rules governing it have changed considerably over the years. In the mid-nineteenth century coroners were elected by the freeholders of the county or borough in which they would serve, rather than being appointed by the local council as they would be from 1888; candidates had to defray their own election expenses. Today the Coroner is a free agent, responsible only to the Lord Chancellor, but then he was under the control of the local justices of the peace with whom he negotiated his salary, though he had the right of appeal to the Home Secretary on this matter. The justices, by and large, were deeply resentful of the coroners, and had more or less openly expressed their determination to suppress the office altogether.[1] The coroner's expenses were a highly contentious subject for, as well as standing expenses such as the pay of his deputy and his clerk, he was obliged to pay medical and other witnesses out of his own pocket directly the inquest was over, reclaiming the amounts later from the borough funds through the justices who paid his salary. Thus both the justices and the counsellors were entitled to examine his accounts, and if they did not agree with him that an inquest had been necessary they could, and not infrequently did, apply the sanction of refusing to reimburse him, despite the fact that the decision as to whether or not to hold an inquest was nominally his responsibility alone. Thus his paymasters had a potent means of keeping the rates down by discouraging the holding of inquests except in the most blatant cases of violence. This situation was attacked regularly by the Registrar General, and Wakley had fought hard for the right of the coroner to be the sole arbiter of whether or not an inquest should be held, uninfluenced by the threat of financial sanctions, but the system would not be changed until after Lankester's death.

The rules governing the registration of births and deaths were also very different in the mid-nineteenth century from those of today. Though at that time the notification of deaths to the Registrar was compulsory, there was no requirement that the certificate be signed by a medical man or necessarily, even if the death had been sudden, that it should be reported to the coroner; the decision on this was that of the Registrar alone. Only in the case of bodies "found exposed" was it compulsory that the coroner be informed. Thus the Registrar, with no medical guidance, was responsible for deciding whether or not the coroner should hear of the vast majority of cases of sudden death. Once notified, it was up to the coroner to decide whether or not to order an inquest, and it was not until this decision was made that he could require a *post mortem* examination of the body. So unless the coroner was medically qualified, the decision on the holding of an inquest was also made in the total absence of any medical guidance.

Wakley had, in fact, been the first medically qualified coroner; previously, all had held legal qualifications. He had had to fight his campaign against the entrenched might of the legal profession, and he had done so on the grounds that only a medical man had the knowledge to enable him to decide whether a death was suspicious. A coroner without such knowledge could easily be prevailed upon to save money by pronouncing meaningless verdicts such as "found drowned", "died of natural causes" or "sudden death". Wakley had only succeeded in winning election at his second attempt, and that after a fierce and expensive struggle in which his brilliance as an orator played an important part. But such was his success in office that on his death, 23 years later, there were no fewer than 59 medically qualified coroners in the country.

It was against this background, of which he must have been well aware, that Lankester allowed himself to be persuaded by members of his own profession to contest the office of Coroner for the Central Division of Middlesex.* Though he was a far less flamboyant character than Wakley, the ideals of the two men were very similar, he greatly admired Wakley's fight, and realized that he was well qualified to carry it on. In addition, as Coroner he would be able to bring greater pressure for action on the

---

* Wakley's district of West Middlesex had apparently been split into the West and Central Divisions on his death.

authorities to right the evils he had first noted as MOH, than he could in the latter office. His path should have been easier than Wakley's, for in 1860 a Parliamentary Select Committee on coroners had recommended that an inquest should he held in every case of sudden death where there was any reason to suspect criminality or where the cause was unknown, and though the recommendation did not become a legal requirement for many years, it considerably strengthened the coroner's hand, though without yet removing the need for a medically trained coroner. The bitterness between the two professions remained, and the fight for Central Middlesex was to be a vicious one.

On 7 June the *Lancet* reported that Wakley's son, Thomas H. Wakley, would be standing as the medical candidate, but he seems to have withdrawn, for the following week only Doctors Lankester and Challice (the MOH for Bermonsey), and a lawyer, Mr. Lewis, were mentioned. On 21 June the *Lancet* called on Dr. Challice to withdraw so as not to split the medical vote, and congratulated him fulsomely the following week for doing so. Throughout the election all three medical weeklies strongly supported Lankester in their editorials, not only as a medical man, but also as a scientist with a trained, analytical mind, the *Lancet*, Wakley's own journal, giving him especially detailed and vociferous coverage. The great William Farr himself published a letter supporting Lankester's candidature, and a volunteer election committee was set up, meeting daily at the candidate's home in Savile Row to collect funds and organize the campaign. Lankester did not, however, receive the support he might have expected from the upper echelons of the profession:

> ... most of those who are fain to claim the title of leaders of the profession, and who do in fact monopolize many of its honours and dignities, showed a cautious and gentleman-like apathy. Some of them consented to "lend their names" to the committee; but with that gracious condescension their activity ended, and this exhausted alike their energies and their liberality ... That the victory was won was due ... not to any councillors or examiners of any of the Colleges of Surgeons, but to the public spirit of several influential general practitioners, the active energy of some younger men who gave mental and physical labour to the cause, and to the warm sympathy and friendliness of the general body of the profession throughout the district.[2]

The election was due to take place on Monday, 7 July, and on 26 June Lankester addressed the "Members of the medical profession" through the columns of the *BMJ*:

> Gentlemen - As this is the last time before the election that I shall have the opportunity of addressing you through the medical press, let me urge upon

you the continuance of your efforts on my behalf. The present contest is not only one between the choice of a medical or legal man for Coroner, but between myself and skilful, practised and unscrupulous electioneering agents. I look to you, who have known me for twenty-five years, to protect me from the cowardly and dastardly attacks of my opponents, and by your personal efforts on my behalf, on Monday, to vindicate my character and that of your profession by doing all that you can to place me at the head of the poll ...

Unfortunately this letter, together with an appeal for help on polling day, was not published until 12 July, but the *Lancet* editorial on 5 July confirmed Lankester's complaint against the legal camp:

Evading the great question of fitness, the most irrelevant, the most gratuitous, and the most unjustifiable efforts have been made, in the supposed interests of a legal candidate, to impugn, not the professional character of the medical candidate, but his personal character.

When the results of the election were finally announced, two days after the polls closed and following a recount requested by Lewis, Lankester had won by 1131 votes to 1084, a majority of 47, so becoming the country's sixtieth medical coroner. The press welcomed the appointment, the *Illustrated London News* publishing his portrait together with an account of his life (Fig. 19). All three medical weeklies united to congratulate him and those members of the profession who had worked so hard and so unstintingly for him against the massed ranks of the legal profession "well versed in election matters and having at their command paid agents".[3] Altogether Lankester's committee raised £180 from the medical profession towards his expenses, and 92 of his own friends subscribed £200 3s 6d between them in sums ranging from 10 guineas to half a guinea, the list being headed by Thomas H. Wakley and including William Hardwicke. However, the campaign cost over £3000 in all, a huge sum in those days, and the balance of over £2600 came out of Lankester's pocket.[4,5] He had no private means, and his finances never recovered from the blow; his affairs were in the hands of the receiver when he died. Some years after the election he was reported as saying to a meeting of the BMA that:

He regarded having obtained the Coronership for Middlesex as one of the great calamities of his life. He did not believe that those who helped him to win this office knew how hardly it had pressed on his resources, but he would warn them against any attempt at pressing a medical brother into so dangerous a position, as that of sustaining the expenses of a county contest

Fig. 42. Dr. Edwin Lankester

for so thankless an office. Even when got without contest, the salary paid is not equal to the service demanded.[1]

Meanwhile, in the Western Division the medical candidate, to the disgust of the *Lancet*, had retired without a struggle, leaving the field to two lawyers. The two divisions, though each now had its own coroner were, together with the Eastern Division, all administered by the same Bench.

Lankester was 48 years old when he was elected to the coronership, and he held the post, together with that of MOH for St. James's, Westminster, until his death. On election he gave up all attempts at private practice, but continued in his post at New College until 1872, using the position during his election campaign to emphasize his qualifications as a scientist as well as a medical man. As far as is known, his income over this period was derived from these three posts and from the books and articles he had written and continued to write, though the "dirty party in St. James's,

Westminster", in a "most indecent piece of economy", sought to "take advantage of [his] election to the office of Coroner to diminish the salary attached to the duties of MOH" by £200.[6] As to his multitude of voluntary jobs, he did not resign from the secretaryship of Section D of the British Association until the following year, and he held various council and committee posts in the Metropolitan Association of MOH until 1869 and in the Social Science Association until 1873. He continued to drive himself to the limit of his strength and beyond until the end.

His first duty as Coroner was to appoint a Deputy, and in this he found no difficulty, for his old friend William Hardwicke, the MOH for Paddington, agreed to act for him. Next he had to find a clerk, an office, and a carriage, all of which had to be paid for out of his salary, as did his Deputy, State papers, and advances to witnesses. He was able to economise on the office by setting it up in his own home in Savile Row. By law, a coroner's salary was calculated at the rate of £1 each for the average number of inquests carried out annually over the previous five years. Expenses were allowed at the rate of 6s 8d per inquest. If the population of the district increased during succeeding years, the salary was increased in proportion, but Lankester complained from the start that when the West Middlesex District was split, the whole of the increase went to the Western Division, he in the Central Division received none of it;[7] on top of which the huge debt he had incurred for election expenses was crippling him financially. On the above basis, his salary had been fixed at £1220 a year, out of which he had to find £200 a year for the carriage and £450 for the other expenses, thus leaving for his own use scarcely £600 a year. As he pointed out, it was "barely the stipend of a chief clerk in a Government Office", and certainly not a sum from which he could afford to advance £450 every six weeks for witnesses.[1] He claimed £1370 as a minimum, and referred the matter to the Middlesex magistrates.

Having made the necessary arrangements for carrying out his duties, Lankester's next move was to join his professional body, the Coroners' Society of England and Wales. This Society had been founded in 1846 and, among other causes which it took up, had given valuable support to the Registrar General in his fight for the independence of the coroners from the judiciary. The membership of the Society was about 90 when Lankester joined, but it had dropped to around 60 ten years later. Only six members were based in, or close to, London, so that it was on these few that the onus of running the Society inevitably devolved. Because the scattered membership made the holding of ordinary meetings impractical, the quarterly committee meetings were open to any member wishing to attend, and printed records of the Annual General Meeting, held in May, were sent to all members. As ever when he joined an organisation, Lankester lost no time in taking an active part in its proceedings. The first

Committee Meeting he attended was in October, 1863, and the last in January, 1872; out of a possible 34 quarterly meetings between these two dates, he attended 26, and at six of these he and the Secretary were the only members present, though the Managing Committee, to which he was elected at his first Annual General Meeting in Meeting in May, 1863, was 14 strong. In fact, committee meetings rarely drew more than four members and Annual Meetings from six to twelve, yet the Society was very active in the coroners' cause, and Lankester was quick to take advantage of its help. In November, 1865, he chaired a general meeting at which the revision of salaries under the Coroners' Act was discussed, and members were given guidance on how to appeal to the Home Secretary if they were not satisfied with their own magistrates' award. The Middlesex coroners had probably already appealed and were sharing their experience with the others, for a year later their affairs were discussed at a Committee Meeting. The Society's minutes make no further mention of the matter, but early in 1867 the *Lancet* reported that Lankester's salary had been raised to £1770, back-dated to the previous January and to run for five years. This was on the basis that he had carried out 1271 inquests in 1863-4, 1246 in 1864-5, and 1385 in 1865-6. His popularity with his magistrates could not have been improved by the award.

Lankester also enlisted the Society's help, though with less success, over another problem. At an inquest on a murder victim, the police had refused him permission to call on the suspected murderer, who was then in their custody, to give evidence, as the Coroner felt he should. When he brought the matter to the Society, it backed his appeal to the Home Office, but permission was again refused on the grounds that, in giving evidence, the prisoner would risk incriminating himself.

Just as he published as widely as possible his Annual Reports as MOH, in order to draw attention to the social evils of the day and the means of remedying them, so Lankester was determined from the first to make similar use of the office of Coroner. It was unusual for coroners to publish such reports, but this did not deter him. The first two, for 1862-3 and 1863-4, appeared as supplements to the *Transactions of the National Association for the Promotion of Social Science,** the third and fourth were printed in Lankester's short-lived *Journal of Social Science,* and the fifth to seventh were again attached to the *Transactions,* the sixth also appearing as a booklet published by Robert Hardwicke. It seems likely that the seventh was the last, for not only have I been unable to trace any others, but no more were noticed in the medical press, as all the first seven were.

---

* I have been unable to trace these, but Lankester himself, in his Third Report, commented on their favourable reception, and the *MTG* reviewed them. [8,9]

In his first Report, Lankester established his reasons for publishing them, reasons which, though they may be taken for granted today, were by no means generally accepted at that time.

It is not alone in the investigation of cases to which criminality is attached that the coroner's court is of importance. It ought to be made the great safeguard of society against the prevalence of any preventable cause of death in our prisons, lunatic asylums and workhouses.[8]

Again, the *BMJ*, discussing Lankester's Third Report wrote:

Dr. Lankester drew attention to the importance of the Coroner's Court in deaths from preventable diseases ... showing that ... there was no doubt that not only the coroner had the power, but that it was his duty to hold inquests in such cases. In many cases of zymotic disease, the cause was so obviously dependent on neglect or deficiency that it was only necessary to draw public attention to the existence of these causes at once, to put an end to the spread of disease ... One of the most powerful aids provided by the law for arresting the spread of preventable disease, was the Coroner's Court.[10]

Here was the coroner's job as seen through the eyes of a MOH, a novel viewpoint which Lankester would exploit again and again. If adopted officially it would have added a whole new dimension to the coronership, never envisaged in the historical context in which it had been instituted, namely the investigation by a knight (i.e., a responsible person) of violent of suspicious deaths.

From the beginning too, as might be expected from so dedicated a popular educator as Lankester, he used his inquests and the reports which they generated in the press to impress on jurors and public alike any lessons in both social and health matters which could be learned from the cases considered. As the *MTG* wrote:

Every inquest he holds is a practical lecture, and because practical more likely to be heeded by the class of persons who for the most part constitute coroners' juries. The doctrine taught, whether sanitary or ethical, comes home to the intelligence of the uneducated, and the repetition of the lesson must in time succeed in fixing it in the mind. From the inquest-room it goes to the public-house parlour, and there it is talked over, and into the shops, and there it is gossiped about, and into the family, and there the wife learns it. Can it be believed that such work carried on earnestly and conscienciously, as Dr. Lankester carries it on, shall fail in producing some impression upon those ranks in society which it is most important to reach, and which it is otherwise so difficult to reach?[11]

And of his Annual Reports it was said:

Nothing can be more interesting than these serious histories of our own times, so short, so closely packed with the sins and sorrows of the very people among whom we live. Dr. Lankester has the happy knack of making his reports readable, and yet so admirably arranged that they are handy as pocket dictionaries.[12]

It was not long before he ran into trouble with one of the vestries in his district. The coroner had the right to nominate a constable in each parish to gather information for him and to deliver his warrants, the constable to be paid by the local justices. In the St. Pancras Vestry Lankester had nominated a Mr. Murray, but for some reason the Vestry took exception to this, wishing him to use their own nominee. When he refused to agree, they dismissed Murray from their service, hoping thus to leave Lankester no alternative but to employ their man. But Murray still remained a constable for the Metropolitan District and Lankester maintained that, as such, he was fully entitled to employ him, which he continued to do. Both sides then set about checking their positions. Lankester successfully obtained the backing of the Coroners' Society for his stand, but Counsel called in by the Vestry found that that body had overstepped its legal rights. The *MTG* congratulated Lankester on fighting for and keeping his independence.

In his First Report (1862-3), Lankester took up the subject of *post mortem* examinations, which he had already raised as MOH in 1858 and 1859, and on which his insistence would later cause serious conflict with his justices. An inquest verdict of "found dead" should, he said, never be countenanced; a *post mortem* should always be performed to clarify the precise reason for the death, and all *post mortems* should be complete. For instance, at an inquest on a woman who had been killed falling downstairs when drunk, the doctor who carried out the *post mortem* had failed to analyse the stomach. Lankester announced that:

he wished it to be distinctly understood by the profession that, when he ordered a *post mortem* examination to be made it was to be a thorough and not a partial one; all the organs were to be tested, as poison had frequently been found where there was no suspicion of anything of the kind.[13]

He returned to the subject in his Second Report (1863-4). At that date there were no experienced Home Office pathologists specialising in *post mortems* on whom the coroner could call, as is the case today. Examinations were carried out by any general practitioner chosen and paid by the coroner. Naturally very few were experienced in the art, and many disliked it intensely and begged to be excused. Lankester foresaw the need for a system such as the modern one when he wrote:

> I should be glad if it could be arranged that all *post mortem* examinations could be made by some one or more gentlemen who had made this subject an especial study, and who, by devoting their whole time to it, would be able to draw up reports which would form not only a valuable contribution to pathology, but would render more satisfactory the conclusions of the coroner's court with regard to the cause of death.[9]

A further problem he noted was that there were no Home Office forensic laboratories (as there are today) where chemical and other analyses could be carried out, duties of which general practitioners were certainly incapable. The *MTG* strongly supported Lankester's views, urging him to express them more fully, which he did in his Fourth Report (1865-6), ending:

> ... what we want for the science of medical jurisprudence is a body of well-reported cases in reference to the inquiries in chemistry, physiology, and morbid anatomy, which come before our courts of law relative to the causes of death.[14]

Here spoke Lankester the scientist. His views were taken very seriously by the Social Science Association, and at a meeting in May, 1867, under the chairmanship of William Farr, he led a discussion on the subject.

Another matter which he had raised as MOH was the need for district mortuaries, particularly to relieve slum-dwellers from the necessity of keeping their dead in their crowded homes until the funeral. Returning to the subject as Coroner[14] he advocated that not only should there be a decent reception room for bodies, but that a *post mortem* room should also be provided, so that examinations could be carried out "fairly easily and effectually", and "the many inconveniences which medical men meet with in making examinations under the present arrangements (such as defiled, dark kitchens and attics in courts and alleys) be avoided, and thus greater accuracy secured". He also suggested that a third room should be added in which inquests could be held, for in this way money could be saved by holding several inquests before the same jury. His plea seems to have been heard at last for, despite the despairing comment of the *MTG* three months later: "But who will bell the cat, and be the first to essay the Quixotic experiment of inducing the London parishes to incur the requisite expenditure?", by the following year he was able to report a decrease in the cost of inquests for just this reason.

In his Second Report, Lankester raised two matters which were of widespread concern at the time and to which he would return again and again - infant deaths, and deaths in workhouses and lunatic asylums. Workhouses already had a very bad name, not only among the poor who might one day be incarcerated in them, but also among the more thoughtful members of the wealthier classes. Lankester himself contended publicly to the Social Science Association that "society had no right to treat paupers ... by confining their food within limits which might in any way affect their health".[15] When an inmate of one of these institutions died, it obviously afforded great protection to the survivors if an inquest were held, and Lankester was liberal in their use, even suggesting that they should be made compulsory or that, at least, all death certificates should be submitted to the coroner before burial took place. As far as possible he put his ideas into practice in his own District, to the great annoyance of his magistrates. Matters came to a head in 1872, again in the troublesome St. Pancras parish, when he insisted on holding inquests into four deaths at its workhouse, and the Guardians complained to the magistrates. The Magistrates' Clerk replied on their behalf that if the Coroner's expenditure on inquests continued at its present level, his masters would complain to the Home Secretary, and would be within their legal rights in refusing to allow the Coroner to speak in his own defence. Lankester was sent a copy of the letter. Taking prompt action on his own behalf, he brought the matter before the court of public opinion by addressing one of his juries on the subject, reminding them of the useful outcome of an inquest he had held three years earlier on an inmate of the same workhouse, after an attempt by the authorities "to screen their improper practices from the public by excluding the action of the Coroner's Court".[16] I have found no record that the magistrates carried out their threat.

As MOH, Lankester had for long been drawing attention to the horrifying infant death rate in his parish, and to the associated question of the registration of births. Extraordinarily, though the national register of births, deaths and marriages had been set up in 1837, the registration of births, though compulsory in Scotland and Ireland, was not yet so in England and Wales. During his vaccination campaigns Lankester had pointed out that until this was rectified the compulsory vaccination Act of 1853 was a dead letter, and similarly it was impossible to investigate infant deaths, including those claimed as still-births, if there was no record of the births. Now, not only in his inquests and annual reports as Coroner, but through the very active part he played in meetings of the influential Social Science Association, he set about remedying this.

In 1863 he led a delegation from the Metropolitan Association of MOH to the Registrar-General (Major General George Graham) asking for regulation of the whole question of the registration of births and deaths; but they received a very half-hearted reply, promising only that the matter would be considered.[17] Some years later, at a meeting of the Social Science Association, Lankester chaired a session on the subject and made a lengthy contribution to the discussion. On still-births he said he believed that many births claimed as such were, in fact, live births in which the children had been murdered by their mothers, and he quoted in evidence the very low rate of still-births in workhouses compared with the high rate outside. Only if still-births were registered, as they were in most other countries, could they be properly investigated. However, when he had spoken to the Registrar-General on the subject, he told his audience, the reply had been that "it would be disagreeable to ladies in high life to have their abortions recorded", and this was why the House of Commons had never dealt with the question.[18]

It was in his Third Report (1864-5) as Coroner (for which he thanked Dr. Hardwicke for preparing the tables), which he read at a meeting of the Social Science Association again under the chairmanship of William Farr, that he tackled in depth the question of infant deaths, returning to it in most of his subsequent reports. In that year the results of inquest verdicts on children of under one year had been:

Natural causes	112
Still-born	20
Suffocation in bed	113
Other accidents	10
Infanticide	61
Unknown causes	14
	330

Of all the 330 inquests, 114 had been on newly born children, and in all cases of infanticide of the newborn, the children had been illegitimate and had been found dead in ponds, ditches or streets where attempts had been made to hide them. But Lankester pointed out that there was a marked difference between verdicts reported by different coroners, reflecting a distinct difference of opinion between them, or perhaps between their juries, on how the newborn came by their deaths. For while the West and Central Middlesex coroners reported that one in four or five of their cases were attributed to wilful murder, the East Middlesex coroner considered this to be so in only one of his 31 cases. Reflecting this, of 203 verdicts of wilful murder of the newborn in the whole of England and Wales that year, no less than 99 had been delivered in Middlesex. It was comparatively easy, he said, to show that a newborn child had been actively killed; the difficulty arose when, as in so many cases, it was allowed to die by wilful neglect; but even here he described distinctive appearances which clearly indicated an intention to kill.

Discussing what could be done to reduce the shocking rate of infanticide, he pointed out that in the vast majority of cases the pregnancy had been hidden and the woman had delivered herself in secret, a state of affairs which was almost impossible for girls living at home or in lodgings, where their condition would inevitably be discovered. The only situation in which they could hide the pregnancy was in domestic service, and it was to girls in this employment that almost all cases of murder of the newborn could be attributed. He therefore urged that:

> the kindly superintendence of young women in domestic service by their mistress would often prevent the concealment of their condition and the temptation to destroy their offspring. It must be obvious to all that the extensive prevalence of such oversight in families would go far to prevent a crime which is most frequently perpetrated, not in the homes of the poor, but in those of the middle and upper classes of society in England.[10]

There were, he said, two great legal difficulties in the way of punishment for the crime; the necessity to prove that the child had been "fully born", for it was not illegal to kill a child which had not entirely left the passages of its mother; and the mandatory death penalty, which juries were reluctant to invoke. To remedy both he recommended changes in the law, and by 1869 he was campaigning strongly for the abolition of the death penalty for infanticide. It was not until 1939 that the offence was specifically defined in law, was distinguished from culpable homicide, and given a maximum punishment of three years imprisonment. Lankester's suggestion at a meeting of the Social Science Association that year that seduction by a male should be made a penal offence was so hotly debated that he withdrew it.

He felt strongly that:

> the law of punishment is not ... the most satisfactory way of preventing crime. Systematic attempts should be made to remove the causes of crime; not in the interests of the children alone, but in the moral and physical interest of the mother herself. Besides, the manifest danger to the life of the woman from secret delivery would be prevented. In several cases where women have been detected after infanticide, they have lost their lives.[10]

Among the remedies which he considered was a change in the bastardy laws to make it much easier to hold the man legally responsible for his offspring; "an improvement in the morality of the sexes", though he offered no suggestion as to how this might be brought about; refuges for expectant and single mothers, which would bring the children up after they were delivered (he refuted the argument that such institutions only condoned immorality); and foundling hospitals, though he pointed out that the mortality from infectious diseases of children in such institutions was appalling. It was not until his Sixth Report (1868-9) that he wrote:

> The question must come before the legislature as to whether the man who seduces a woman for his pleasure, is allowed to go free, while she has to bear all the consequences of their joint immorality.[19]

The Social Science Association, meeting in Bristol in 1869, held a session on infanticide at which Lankester read the opening paper, "Can infanticide be diminished by legislative enactment?" Other speakers expressed similar views to his, but none was so sympathetic to the plight of the women as the Lady Superintendent of the Great Coram Street Children's Home in London. Fifteen members contributed to the discussion, including Bristol-born Elizabeth Blackwell, the first woman in England to be registered as a doctor (though she had qualified in the United States), and Mary Carpenter, the great Bristol philanthropist famed for her work for the rehabilitation of delinquent children. Of all the participants only two, both of them clerics, considered that the blame lay entirely with the women, who should be subjected to the full rigours of the law. In the end the meeting recommended that the death penalty for "infanticide at the time of the birth by the mother" should be discontinued, that still-births should be registered, and that the statistics of newborn children found dead in the street should be published. The responsibility of the fathers had been discussed by many speakers, but the only allusion to the subject made in the recommendations was a note to the effect that "many of the members" considered that asylums for the women and their children should be set up and that the state should have authority "to proceed against parents" for maintenance for the children.

Though there was general agreement among the more thoughtful members of society with Lankester's views on the causes of infanticide and its unacknowledged frequency, there were some who felt he went a little too far in his attempts at publicity for the cause. When a papal delegate concluded, from reading the Coroner's estimated figures for infanticide in the country as a whole (which Lankester had extrapolated from those for Middlesex), that England was the infanticide centre of Europe, the *MTG* took him to task for sensationalism on the grounds that city figures were not applicable to the countryside.

Lankester often returned in his Reports to ignorance as an important cause of death, especially of the deaths of children. A case in point was the custom of baby-farming whereby poor mothers, particularly the mothers of illegitimate children who had no husband to support them, handed their infants over to baby-minders while they were out at work. The minders, usually through ignorance but sometimes deliberately, half-starved the children or gave them quite unsuitable food, resulting in a terrible death rate. Again, it was as MOH in 1859 that he had first drawn attention to the extraordinary number of deaths of young children by "suffocation in bed", and he returned to the subject in his 1864-5 Coroner's Report. He suggested five causes for the 113 such deaths which had occurred that year: ignorance, carelessness, overcrowding, over work and drunkenness, the last three being the outcome of poverty. 25% of the cases which came before the courts were due to drunkenness, many infants having been "found dead on a Sunday morning, and I fear many of them are caused by Saturday night orgies". But infant deaths were not confined to the lower classes, ignorance was a major cause.

> If the money that is in many cases spent in teaching young women to play the piano, were spent in giving them a good domestic education, in teaching them as to the nature of pure air, and the proper treatment of children, many of the cases of suffocation would be prevented, as well as a host of diseases by which the lives of children are now sacrificed. I feel, therefore, that while we should endeavour to improve the habits of the lower classes with a view to lessening infant mortality, that we must also give sound instruction to all classes of the community on the laws of life.[20]

Throughout his time as coroner, Lankester used his office to urge the vital importance of public education in health matters, and he himself continued to publish educational books until the end of his life. On Food (Chapter 11) appeared in 1864, and Good Food and How to Get It* in 1867: in 1868 he published Vegetable Physiology, in which he emphasized the need to base all physiological teaching on physics and chemistry, and recapitulated much of his previous popular account of the subject, adding a section on Schleiden and Schwann's recent discovery of the cellular structure of plants and animals. But more influential than any of these were his Practical Physiology: Being a School Manual of Health for the Use of Classes and General Reading (1868), which had run to six editions by 1876, and a booklet addressed to school authorities entitled What shall we Teach? or Physiology in Schools (1870). In addition, an article in Nature[21] pleaded

---

* I have been unable to see this book as the British Library copy has been destroyed.

for the appointment of scientists to school boards. *What Shall we Teach?* had originally been intended as a paper for the Bristol meeting of the Social Science Association where, in the event, the author had been fully occupied by the session on infanticide. It was an expanded version of the Introduction to *Practical Physiology* in which he wrote categorically:

> I wish to state my conviction as a physiologist that there is no anatomical distinction between the brains of men and women, or those of rich and poor people. With regard to education, it appears to me that whatever is of advantage to the rich man is also of advantage to the poor man ... I would even go further and say that which is good for the male is good for the female.

These were advanced views indeed for the time, and held by only a minority of the more progressive thinkers. Continuing on this theme, Lankester pointed out that it was women, not men, who ran the home and the children and on whom, therefore, the good health of the family depended. Hence it was of far more importance that women were educated in health matters than men, and it was vital that the instruction should begin at school, another revolutionary idea at a time when girls were taught little more than the three R's, religion and needlework.

> Half the population of every town in England die before it is five years old, and half this death arises from want of knowledge on the part of mothers and nurses how to feed children,

he wrote (ungrammatically) in *What shall We Teach?*, adding that middle class schools were as neglectful of health education as were those for the working classes. Health education in schools must have been much on his mind at the time, for he also raised the subject in his Annual Report to the Vestry of St. James's in his capacity as MOH.

In his Coroner's Reports, Lankester directed attention to many problems other than workhouse and infant deaths. He discussed suicides, street accidents (there were 200 fatal accidents in London alone in 1865-6); deaths due to "natural causes", including diseases undoubtedly due to excessive drinking; and deaths from unknown causes, a verdict which, he suggested, was often due to the inexperience of the doctor undertaking the *post mortem*, and which led to his call for the employment of experienced pathologists.

In the middle of 1866, before he knew that his salary was to be raised, Lankester became involved in a vicious battle with the Middlesex magistrates both on that subject, and on medical witnesses and their cost to the ratepayers. It seems to have been provoked by a letter to the *Times* in May from Mr. Kemshead, JP., the chairman of the Committee of Accounts responsible for paying him, in which he accused Lankester of deliberately holding unnecessary inquests for the sole purpose of raising his salary. Kemshead cited the example of a terrible accident in Regent's Park in which 38 people were drowned and Lankester insisted on holding a separate inquest on each. The *Lancet* came out with a blistering editorial in the Coroner's defence, claiming that Kemshead might perhaps be excused for his remarks on the grounds of his ignorance of a coroner's duties, but that he could never be forgiven for his charge of dishonesty. At the next magistrates' meeting Kemshead returned to the attack, raising the question of the expense incurred by Lankester's extravagant use of medical witnesses, and coupling it with a bitter complaint of delay in the payment of those witnesses. Lankester disposed of the first complaint by pointing out that Mr. Humphreys, the legally qualified coroner for East Middlesex, called nearly as many medical witnesses as he did, but that Humphrey's expenses were lower because the Middlesex Hospital was in his district and many of his cases were taken there before they died: the *post mortems* were then performed by the hospital doctors who were paid nothing extra for the service. The accusation of delay in the payment of witnesses, Lankester contended, concerned only one case, albeit a highly publicized one. A Dr. Sansome, with whom he had had a private quarrel over a genuine misunderstanding about a two guinea fee, had taken him to court and won his case. At the same meeting Mr. Kemshead was, unfortuately for him, obliged to vindicate Lankester further by reading out a letter from another medical witness complaining of grave delays in payment by Mr. Humphreys while Dr. Lankester always paid promptly. All this was reported in the *Times* in a manner grossly biassed against Lankester (perhaps the Editor still remembered the episode of the death of the seam-stress), and was followed by a spirited correspondence both in that newspaper and in the *Lancet* between Lankester and Sansome, abetted by the Islington Medical Society (for Sansome) and a group of St. Marylebone doctors (for Lankester). The two sides eventually made their peace.

However, in his last letter, on 4 July, Lankester took the opportunity to raise once more his continuing complaint that he had never received the 6s 8d per inquest allowed by law to cover his expenses, adding:

> I have yet to learn ... what claim the magistrates have on me to pay medical witnesses at the time of the inquest when they refund me only once in six weeks.

The infuriated magistrates convened a court a few weeks later at which Lankester unrepentantly repeated his statement, and also flatly denied the *Times*'s charge that he never paid his medical witnesses, producing receipts from those gentlemen for 76 out of the 77 cases he had heard, the missing one being that of Dr. Sansome. Six months later Lankester was notified of the back-dated salary increase granted by the Home Secretary.

Throughout his entire career as Coroner the Middlesex magistrates harried Lankester over his expenses, as they had done Baker[22] and Wakley[23] before him. In May, 1873, the *MTG* published a fighting article in his defence, followed in June by the *Lancet*. The latter, in an annotation entitled "Dr. Lankester and the Middlesex magistrates", suggested that the Bench's accusations would be more convincing if, instead of comparing the average costs of Lankester's and Humphrey's inquests, they were to specify the particular inquests for which Lankester had ordered unnecessary *post mortems*. A few months later, returning to the charge in a piece with the reverse title, "The Middlesex magistrates and Dr. Lankester", it commented:

> Once a quarter without fail, complaints are made of Dr. Lankester's accounts ... [His] inquests cost £2 11s 8d each, a sum so small it is really surprising how justice can be satisfied for the money. It is high time for the "economists" upon the magisterial bench to recognize this fact, and to desist from harassing an energetic officer while discharging his duties.[24]

At the end of 1867 the coronership for West Middlesex fell vacant. Two medical candidates put their names forward, William Hardwicke, who had acted as Lankester's deputy since the latter's appointment in 1862, and a Dr. Diplock. In January, 1868, a meeting was held on the *Lancet*'s premises to decide which man the profession should be recommended to support, so avoiding splitting the medical vote. Hardwicke was prepared to defray all the necessary election expenses and was chosen unanimously, but Lankester, in the light of his own bitter experience, wrote a long letter to the *BMJ* appealing for a simplification of the election procedure so that the ruinous expense resulting from a contested election could be avoided. In the same issue of the *BMJ* a defiant Dr. Diplock announced his continued intention of standing, as he had the organization and the promise of support which were vital to success. There does not seem to have been a legal candidate, and on 29 February it was announced that Dr. Diplock had won by 1503 votes to 1482, despite a re-count demanded by Dr. Hardwicke. Each candidate had spent approximately £1400 on the contest. Shortly afterwards Hardwicke, backed by the *Lancet*, announced his intention of taking Diplock to court on the grounds that:

> a great number of his supporters "illegally voted" for him - that is, they had no legal freehold in the county, many of them having "property in graves" or being "watermen on the Thames".[25]

In an age when property was of supreme importance in defining the franchise, strict rules as to the amount necessary to qualify for a vote were essential to prevent the farcical situations described above. Such rules had already been promulgated by Parliament for national and local elections, but they had not been extended to the election of coroners so that, although Hardwicke doubtless had the necessary evidence to bring his case, he stood little chance of winning it; he may well have brought it primarily for publicity reasons. He was supported by the subscriptions of his fellow doctors (most gave one or two guineas, though Lankester gave ten), but presumably lost his case, for Diplock retained the coronership. Nevertheless, all three medical weeklies began to campaign on regularising the franchise, Lankester referred to the problem in a number of his reports and in contributions to meetings of the Social Science Association, and in 1870 a bill started on its way through Parliament confining the franchise for the election of coroners to those on the Parliamentary voters' roll for the district.

Lankester took an active interest in two other reforms he considered essential for coroners and their courts. In his Fifth Report (1866-7) he drew attention to the fact that there was no law on the constitution of coroners' juries; the coroner could empanel anyone he wished, and no care was taken to see that all those who were liable to serve were called in turn. Also, in 1867 he and four others formed a delegation from the Coroners' Society to the Home Secretary seeking arrangements for retirement pensions. The Home Secretary was sympathetic, but required details as to the expense which would be involved. These were supplied, members lobbied their members of parliament, the Society wrote to Sir George Grey, who replied that he would give the matter his attention "with the disposition to do what was just and equitable". But no Member could be found willing to take charge of the necessary bill, and eventually the proposal had to be dropped.

By 1869 Lankester's continual confrontation with his magistrates, the vestries and other authorities local and national, for the ways and means to carry out his duties in what he believed to be a just and adequate manner, seem to have exhausted his patience, for he wrote in his Report:

> During the seven years to which my reports relate, I am not aware that in any one instance have measures been adopted for the prevention of acknowledged evils, which are obviously under the control of local or general legislation.[26]

Commenting on this, the *MTG* wrote:

Undeterred by that which would have daunted a less earnest and indefatigable public officer, Dr. Lankester is again in the field, urging upon the Legislature and the public reforms and improvements in the Coroner's Court which every unbiassed person must regard as of the utmost importance to the safety of the public and the proper administration of justice.[26]

This is probably as fair a summary of his tenure of office as any.

Chapter Thirteen

Overwork and Anxiety   1868-1874

Lankester had never had any ordered working method, any way of organizing all the multifarious activities he undertook; and there is no doubt that he attempted much more than any one man was capable of doing thoroughly. He was perpetually torn between, on the one hand, his struggle for justice for the underpriviledged, for the diffusion of scientific knowledge among the lay public of all classes, and for the reform of his own profession; and on the other, his devotion to natural science in general and to botany in particular. His difficulty in reconciling these divergent interests was compounded by his continual state of personal financial crisis, especially after the election battle for the coronership, and by the harassment of the Middlesex magistrates over the way in which he carried out his duties as Coroner.

Possibly it was a combination of these factors which resulted in his somewhat acrimonious resignation from the Linnean Society in 1868. It may be remembered that some 12 years earlier he had been in trouble with the Society for failing to pay his annual subscription. Now he was again two years in arrears and the Secretary wrote him a restrained but determined reminder, adding in a postscript that he understood that Lankester had "some idea of withdrawing from the Society"; if this were true, he wrote, the rules insisted on a formal letter of resignation accompanied by all arrears of subscriptions. A few days later Phebe Lankester replied on her husband's behalf enclosing a cheque "with the intimation that this is the *last* he will pay", and a request that the Secretary would "be so good as to recieve this *notice of withdrawal* from the Society". The letter ends strangely; "We should have been glad should Dr. Lankester's entrance fee paid long ago have been made available for our son E. Ray Lankester who may one day ask to be made an FLS".[1] In fact, Ray did become a Fellow in 1875, but not without considerable controversy.[2] It may well be that Phebe assumed the role of secretary to her husband at about this time, for there is one other known occasion on which she intervened in his affairs, and Edwin certainly had need of someone to bring some order into his life.

For whatever reason Lankester resigned from the Linnean Society, he had effectively cut almost his last link with the world of natural science which he loved so much, for Ray would take over as sole editor of the *Quarterly Journal of Microscopical Science* in 1871, and by the end of 1872 he had lost his last teaching appointment, that at New College, as well. His original appointment had been as Professor, at a salary of £200 a year, but at the end of the 1863 session this changed and he became a Lecturer at £100 a year. There is no clue as to the reason for his demotion, but it appears to have been with his agreement, and it seems possible that he himself had asked to be relieved of some of his responsibilities in view of his new duties as Coroner. Nevertheless, he had been teaching at the College since 1850, so it must have come as a considerable shock when he received a letter from the Chairman terminating his appointment because of drastic alterations in staffing due to the resignation of two professors. Lankester did not reply for a fortnight, due to "circumstances which have engaged the whole of my time and attention". He was clearly very upset, pointing out that he had "made many sacrifices to continue my lectures there", and he could not understand why he had been picked on to resign when two other staff members had not, especially as the letter suggested that no personal feelings were involved. He also pointed out that at least half the contents of the museum were his own property, and demanded to meet the Council over the whole matter.

The Secretary replied that "the very unpleasant duty is cast upon me, of communicating the enclosed resolution ... Such a duty is perhaps best performed in as few words as possible". The resolution stated flatly that the Council did not feel at liberty to reopen a question which was already decided, and must decline a personal interview with Lankester. It would, however, appoint a small committee, two members of which had not attended the original Council Meetings, to discuss Lankester's claim to part of the museum exhibits. This completely failed to satisfy Lankester, who replied in a letter "expressed in very strong terms ... complaining of Council refusing to meet him". Eventually he was admitted to an interview and a very unpleasant session took place over which the Minutes draw a discreet veil.

However, as when he was dismissed from the Food Museum, he now began to dispute the amount of money owed to him, the College eventually granting him the £25 which he claimed, but refusing to admit liability. A month later the Secretary informed him that the members of the Committee who would meet him to discuss his claims on the museum had demanded that he first supply them with a list of the objects to which he laid claim, something which he had still failed to do three months later although the College Secretary had tried to help him by supplying him with receipts for the objects which had already been bought from him.

Phebe then further complicated matters by paying on her husband's behalf for some plates made for the College by Lankester's publisher, Robert Hardwicke. When she sent the receipted bill to the College, the authorities not unnaturally demurred, for they did not know whether the plates would eventually be included in Lankester's bill. In her reply to the College, Phebe indicated that her husband's list should soon be forthcoming, but that it was difficult to list and price natural objects which he had simply picked up and deposited in the museum over a period of 20 years. There is no record of the outcome of these transactions.[3]

To judge by his homes at this time, there is little to indicate that Lankester was in the serious financial trouble which must, in fact, have been the case. In 1867 he had moved his London home and the Coroner's Office from Savile Row to 23, Great Marlborough Street and leased a second house in Child's Hill, Hampstead, calling it Melton House after the village where he was born.* Just at the time when his quarrel with New College was at its height he moved from Child's Hill to 68, Belsize Park, Hampstead, an imposing detached residence which still stands. It is a large, double-fronted, three-storeyed building with a basement and a narrow front garden. There is a large bay window on each side of the double front door, which is protected by a square, pillared porch and reached by a flight of ten steps (Fig. 43). It is not the home of a man in financial difficulties, but on the other hand, he had a large family most of whom were still living at home, and the need sometimes to escape from the unceasing problems of his two demanding jobs in central London must have been overwhelming.

At the end of May, 1873, it was Lankester's sad duty to preside at the inquest on the eldest son of his old acquaintance, Mordecai Cooke. The boy, 11-year old Harry Linneus, had been killed falling from the cross-bar of a swing in the playground of his private school, and as Cooke was abroad at the time, it had fallen to his wife to attend the inquest in his stead. As always, Lankester conducted it with marked consideration for the bereaved, his genial face and portly form helping to put the grieving woman and nervous young witnesses at their ease. True to his reputation, his enquiries were extremely thorough, for he not only assured himself, by questioning Harry's schoolmates, that the child had fallen accidentally from the swing and had not been pushed, but also that the medical attention he had received immediately after the accident was as prompt and competent as was possible in the circumstances.[4]

---

*Child's Hill apparently referred to the district, not to a specific road, for by 1872 the address had become more precise, changing to Burgess Hill, Finchley Road, Hampstead. Only one Victorian house still stands in Burgess Hill, a single-fronted, three-storeyed building of no great presence, which may have been typical of the road.

Fig. 43. 68, Belsize Park, Hampstead, Edwin Lankester's last home (1989).

Lankester's health must already have been beginning to deteriorate at the time of the inquest on Harry Cooke, for the following month the Vestry of St. James's granted him up to five weeks sick leave from his duties as MOH, William Hardwicke, his opposite number in Paddington, having agreed to stand in for him. As Hardwicke was already Lankester's Deputy Coroner, and would be acting for him in that capacity as well, he must have been very stretched for those five weeks. Lankester was suffering from diabetes for which there was, at that date, no known treatment, but despite this he not only continued in his two salaried posts for another year, but even found time to continue publishing in a small way.

Haydn's *Dictionary of Popular Medicine and Hygiene* (1874) boasted the marvellous subtitle, "Comprising all possible self-aids in accident and disease: being a companion for the Traveller, Emigrant and Clergyman, as well as for the heads of all families and institutions". It had been arranged and planned before Lankester, "assisted by Eminent Members of the Royal Colleges of Physicians and Surgeons" undertook to edit it, and though he was very much in sympathy with its aim of instructing the public in the laws of health, he only agreed to do so if he was allowed to insert a section on public health. His 16-page Introduction consisted of a strong plea for preventive medicine together with a short history of the medical profession, including his usual virulent attack on homoeopathy, but for the first time this was tempered with the remark:

> nevertheless ... they have taught us that many diseases will get well of their own accord if due attention be paid to those first necessaries of healthful existence ... This is the lesson we read, and the instruction we derive, from homoeopathy.

His last publication continued his efforts at health education. He revised and republished (with Robert Hardwicke) five of his now well known foolscap leaflets of "Sanitary Instructions", priced at 1d each or 30s per thousand. They covered: "Plain rules for the management of infants", "On the Nature of Scarlet Fever and the best means of preventing it", "Smallpox and its prevention", "Precautions against Cholera and Diarrhoea", and "Measles and its prevention" (Fig. 36). On the backs of those dealing with infectious diseases was printed a summary of the law on the prevention of their spread as defined in the 1866 Sanitary Act, which included the imposition of a £5 fine for wilfully or negligently spreading a disease, and a command to cab-drivers to refuse suspicious fares.

From quite early in 1874, Lankester began to suffer from a series of carbuncles (boils) which necessitated his periodic absence from the coroner's court and his other duties. He was placed in the care of two well known physicians but matters did not improve so, at the beginning of October, after writing to St. James's Vestry to apologise for his absence, he went to stay at 7, The Paragon, Margate. There "it was announced that the bracing air was doing the Coroner good".[5] On 15 October the Vestry reported Lankester's continued absence to the Sanitary Committee for its consideration. But by the end of the month he was seriously ill, the carbuncles spread, his joints swelled, a generalised infection set in, and on 30 October he died. His eldest son, Ray, signed his death certificate and his body was brought back to London to be buried not, as might have been expected in a Non-Conformist burial ground, but in the Cemetery of Hampstead Parish Church. Even as he lay dying the Middlesex magistrates were haggling over one of his inquests. As to the Vestry, after the entry in the Minutes of 15 October, there is no further mention of their MOH of 18 years standing until 12 November, when his death is mentioned in a passing reference to the fact that William Hardwicke would continue to stand in for him for the time being. There are no tributes, no regrets, no sympathy for the family, nothing.

His simple will, which he had drawn up in 1857, was proved on 3 December, and in it he named his wife as executrix and sole legatee. However, his total effects, which came to under £2000 with "leaseholds", the latter presumably on his houses in Great Marlborough Street and Belsize Park, were immediately seized by the Receiver. We know this because the Vestry Minutes for 26 November state that the one month's salary due to him was to:

> be paid to the receiver of his estate on behalf of his creditors; and under the circumstances ... the sum of £25 for the remainder of this quarter's salary as Medical Officer of Health, and the quarter's salary as Analyst which would have been due to him at Christmas next, viz. £12 10s, be allowed to his widow.

His financial affairs had never recovered from the fight for the coronership 12 years earlier.

Lankester's obituarists were united in praising his "geniality of temperament, amiability of disposition and kindness of heart, which endeared him to a large circle of friends".[6] They also noted that he took on far too many responsibilities for one man, and that though he was a prodigious worker, his complete lack of method resulted in the burden of his offices being far greater than it need have been. The medical journals all extolled his conduct of the coronership, the *Lancet* going so far as to assert that "his inquests and his reports were more considered and regarded than those of any other coroner in England, save those of his predecessor [Wakley]", and they all condemned out of hand the behaviour of the Middlesex magistrates, the *Lancet* remarking that he was "faithful unto death" in fighting their "stinginess". There were, however, some curious omissions. Only the *BMJ* laid emphasis on the importance of his work in public health and education, and none of the obituaries made any mention of his extensive intervention in medical politics in the 1850s, an omission which is especially curious in the case of the *BMJ*, the organ of the British Medical Association in the birth of which he played so large a part.

The *Quarterly Journal of Microscopical Science*,[7] as would be expected, commented at length on the more scientific aspects of Lankester's career.

> He was a born naturalist, and not one of those whose love of natural objects is fostered by academical ambition ... But while he was a diligent observer of nature he was also something beyond, and was never satisfied with the easy standard of excellence set up by those who pride themselves on the name of field naturalists.

While commenting on his unceasing efforts to popularise science, and especially microscopy, by means of his lectures and popular books, the writer (J.F.P.) considered that:

> the production of many of them [books] must have been due to circumstances rather than predilection; and while the energy which they display is astonishing, we may be tempted to regret that so much of it was thus directed. We cannot doubt that Dr. Lankester himself might sometimes have found more congenial occupation in strictly scientific research.

It is doubtless true that the income from his writings and talks was very necessary in his straitened financial circumstances, but studying his life today it is difficult to agree with J.F.P. that scientific research was Lankester's real bent; for the experimental work which he carried out early in his career, before he had too many other commitments, did not show any great originality and, though he was undoubtedly especially interested in the chemistry and biology of water, he became superficially interested in a wide variety of unconnected subjects, studying none in depth. As both MOH and Coroner, on the other hand, he threw all his talents and his selfless energy into the single cause, the battle for the health and welfare of the people, especially of the poor. He was a born reformer, teacher and publicist who found satisfaction and fulfilment in his duties, marred only by the continued obstruction of his authorities. He organized inspections, collected statistics, and brought pressure to bear on his Vestry to take action on the evils which he found; he published and publicised his annual reports, both as MOH and as Coroner, using the latter position to reinforce his work as MOH; he lectured and published leaflets and popular books on health matters, and helped to bring pressure on the Government by his active participation in the affairs of his professional societies. If the Public Health Act had not come into force in 1856, so opening up a new career in medicine to men who had been excluded from membership of the Royal College of Physicians, Lankester might well have become a scientist, thus fulfilling John Lindley's ambitions for him, for it is clear that the existing medical posts which would have been open to him had little appeal. However, if this had happened it is my belief that, though his life might well have been less traumatic, less stressful and longer, he would have felt a personal frustration at his inability either to reach the top as a scientist, or to satisfy the caring side of his nature by using his gifts in the service of his fellow men.

Why was his important contribution to the public health movement only mentioned in one obituary, and the part he played in the Broad Street cholera outbreak not at all? Why had his forceful intervention in the founding of the British Medical Association and in the negotiations preceding the Medical Reform Act fallen so soon into oblivion? Lankester's tragedy was that his ideas were before their time. He was by no means the only man (or woman) to see what was wrong with Victorian society and to be well aware of what steps should be taken to put matters right; how to force action from the authorities was another matter. It was not until years after his death, in some cases not until the twentieth century, that the consciences of the country's rulers and of the moneyed classes were sufficiently stirred to put human values before personal gain, at least when they recognized that a healthy and contented employee was better value than a sickly one. Before that happened, Lankester had been driven to a premature death by overwork, anxiety and the persecution of the Middlesex magistrates.

There seem to be two other reasons why Lankester's work as MOH and in medical politics were forgotten by the time of his death. It is one of the injustices of history that a famous son obliterates the memory of his father. Ray Lankester was a brilliant scientist who rightly eclipsed his father in that field, but somehow expunged his memory as medical man and reformer as well, so that when Edwin is remembered at all, it is as the father of Ray. Secondly, one can only suppose that the controversial nature of his coronership and his fame as a popular educator so overshadowed his more enduring work, that even at his death the important part played by this dedicated man in the social and medical reforms of his century was all too soon forgotten.

Postscript

On Lankester's death the post of Coroner for Central Middlesex once again became a battleground fought over by a lawyer and a medical man. William Hardwicke, who had been Lankester's deputy throughout his tenure of the post and was acting for him when he died, eventually won the vicious struggle by, it was first thought, 300 votes, though this was reduced to 255 on a recount. The *Lancet* regarded the victory as a sign that:

> the public ... has little sympathy with the niggardliness of the Middlesex magistrates who were always harrassing Dr. Lankester ... about unnecessary inquests, and still more about unnecessary *post mortem* examinations.[1]

Indeed, this must have been the case, for the public was well aware that if it elected a lawyer the rates would probably be lower. Hardwicke was not quite of Lankester's calibre but he was, nevertheless, just as committed to his predecessor's ideals, working tenaciously to uncover the whole truth at his inquests and, as MOH for Paddington (for he had retained that post), to promote health and social progress in his parish. He only held the Coronership for seven years, succumbing to a stroke in 1881 at the age of 64.

Phebe Lankester (Fig. 44) was 49 when her husband died, but she was a woman of independence and great strength of character, fully capable of organizing her own life. She moved from Hampstead to central London, making her home at 5, Wimpole Street, and there she lived with her two unmarried daughters, Fay and Nina, and her youngest son, Owen, until her death. She had a real flair for writing and produced several more popular books, not only on botany but on health matters too, all delightfully written. Sadly, they were no longer published by Robert Hardwicke, for he had died following a stroke in 1875, at the early age of 53. (The Hardwicke family was subject to strokes). The financial affairs of his firm were in chaos at his death, due to the mounting costs of the illustrations for *English Botany* (the series for which Phebe had written the popular sections), which proved to be too great a burden for so small a firm.

As well as writing books, Phebe produced for 20 years a highly successful weekly column for women, under the pen-name "Penelope", which was syndicated to East Anglian and other provincial newspapers. Such articles, or chats, covering passing events and matters of general

Fig. 44. Mrs. Phebe Lankester, from a painting by H. Herkomer.

interest, were an innovation at the time and proved very popular. Through her writing she made a wide circle of friends including painters, actors and writers. Towards the end of her life her mind began to fail, and she died in April, 1900 and was buried with her husband.[2]

Seven of the eleven Lankester children survived to adulthood. Fay, the eldest, continued her father's work in health education in one of the few ways then open to women, by joining the National Health Association. This organisation, open to both sexes, was founded in about 1872:

> to unite and organise voluntary efforts for the collection and diffusion of well-established sanitary knowledge, which bears on the physical and moral welfare of all classes of society.[3]

It had branches all over the country the purpose of which was to work both with the existing sanitary authorities and with families and households. Fay became its Secretary in 1881 and was still holding the post in 1895, the date of the last surviving Annual Report.

It is impossible to write a brief résumé of the life of Sir Edwin Ray Lankester (Sir Ray), the brilliant eldest son named after the great botanist his father admired so much (Fig. 45). Like Edwin, he was a large, impressive and charming man with a great sense of humour, though his impetuous temperament could lead him into unfortunate quarrels. He inherited, too, his father's booming voice and brilliance as a teacher. Benefitting from an excellent education, he so far outshone Edwin academically that his contribution to zoology has eclipsed in posterity's short memory the major part his father played in public health and social affairs. Yet Ray learned his passion for nature from Edwin, and the two were close friends, working together on such projects as the editorship of the *Quarterly Journal of Microscopical Science.* Ray was fascinated by every branch of the animal kingdom, publishing important papers on, among many other subjects, the embryology of the Mollusca, the malaria parasite, blood corpuscles, the fish heart and the brain of the monkey. Among the posts which he held were the Chair of Zoology at University College, London, (his father's *alma mater*), the Linacre Chair of Comparative Anatomy at Oxford, and the Directorship of the Natural History Museum; and he himself founded the Marine Biological Association and its Laboratories at Plymouth. As well as his knighthood, he received scientific honours too numerous to mention. Ray achieved in zoology all that others had hoped that Edwin would achieve in botany.

Little is known of most of the remaining children. Samuel Rushton (Rushton was Phebe's mother's maiden name), whose date of birth is not given even on his memorial stone in Hampstead Cemetery, became British Consul in Batavia, Dutch East Indies, where he died in 1921, leaving a large family. One of his sisters, Nina, became the head of a Post Office department; another, probably Jessie, married the Rev. Vatcher, a clergyman in the East End of London, and took an active part in philanthropic work[4]. Edward Forbes (1855-1934), named after Edwin's friend, the founder of the Red Lion Club, was called to the Bar in 1878, practised in Common Law and before Parliamentary Committees, and then in 1921 became a police magistrate in West London.[5] The youngest son, Alfred Owen (1859-1933), who was known as Owen, and named after the great zoologist, was a general practitioner working from his mother's home in Wimpole Street. Like Ray, he bore a close resemblance to his father and had all the latter's charm. A delightful obituary notice in the *Lancet* remarks that he was:

Fig. 45. Sir Ray Lankester.

... one of the last of the Victorian family physicians remaining in active practice ... His laugh was the most infectious I have ever heard, and it came from a heart which radiated a kindness and a tolerance and a love for his fellow men, which were as genuine as they are rare.[6]

It was Owen's daughter who gave to Ipswich Museum (of which Ray was at one time President) the portrait of Phebe which had hung over her father's sitting-room mantlepiece (Fig. 45).[4] The Lankesters must have been a delightful family, for all the surviving obituaries emphasize their kindliness, good nature and charm.

References

Abbreviations

AMJ	*Association Medical Journal*
BAAS	British Association for the Advancement of Science
BMJ	*British Medical Journal*
DNB	*Dictionary of National Biography*
MTG	*Medical Times and Gazette*
QJMSc	*Quarterly Journal of Microscopical Science*
TNAPSSc	*Transactions of the National Association for the Promotion of Social Science*

Chapter 1. Suffolk Childhood

General sources: Anon. (1874). Edwin Lankester, M.D., M.R.C.P., F.R.S. *Lancet*, **2**, 676.
Anon. (1903). Lankester, Edwin (1814-1874). *DNB*, **11**, 578.

1. Glyde, J. *The Autobiography of a Suffolk Farm Labourer*, p. 17. Printed article in a collection of "Materials for a History of Woodbridge". Held in Woodbridge Public Library.
2. Phillimore, Blagg and Taylor (Eds) (1912). *Suffolk Parish Registers*.
3. Register of Burials, Quay Street Congregational Chapel, Woodbridge.
4. Weaver, C. and Weaver, M. (1987). *The Seckford Foundation*. Woodbridge: Seckford Foundation.
5. Harrington, J. R., Woodbridge Public Library. Personal communication.

Chapter 2. Physician in Training

General sources. Holloway, S. W. F. (1964). Medical Education in England, 1830-1858: a Sociological Analysis. *History, 49,* 299.
Newman, C. (1957). *The Evolution of Medical Education in the Nineteenth Century.* O.U.P.

1. Smith, F. B. (1979). *The People's Health,* 1830-1910. Croom Helm, 375.
2. Pole, L. (1985). Stand Awhile and Admire. A History of the Saffron Walden Museum. *Occasional Journal of the Saffron Walden Historical Society,* **28.**
3. National Census, 1851.
4. Anon. (1888). Great Natural History Collections: Saffron Walden Museum. *Life Lore,* 104.
5. Bellot, H. H. (1929). *University College, London. 1826-1926.* U. L. Press.
6. Lankester, E. (1841). Letter 3641, College Correspondence. Held in Archives of University College, London.
7. Lankester, E. (1836). Essay on the Uncertainty of Medical Science. *Lond. Med. Surg. J.,* **2,** 468-476.
8. G. S. B. (1909). Lindley, John (1799-1865). *DNB,* **12,** 277.
9. University College, London (1828-1839). *Distribution of Prizes. Examination Papers.* Held in Archives of University College, London.
10. Cope, Z. (1959). *The Royal College of Surgeons of England. A History.* London: Blond.

Chapter 3. Building a Career

General source. Peterson, M. J. (1978). *The Medical Profession in Mid-Victorian London.* University of California Press.

1. Lankester, E. (1849). Application for physiciancy at University College Hospital. College Correspondence. Held in Archives of University College, London.
2. Charlton, B. (1949). *The Recollections of a Northumbrian Lady, 1815-1866.* London: Cape.
3. *Doncaster Gazette,* 1837-1839. News items.
4. Lankester, E. (1842). *An Account of Askern and its Mineral Springs.* London

5. Lankester, E. (1837). Letter No. 4128, dated 18 October, College Correspondence. Held in Archives of University College London.
6. Sillett, R. E. W. (1956). *Edwin Lankester*. Thesis for the Degree of M.D. in the University of Birmingham.
7. Anon. (1874). Edwin Lankester, M.D., M.R.C.P., F.R.S.. *Lancet*, 2, 676.
8. Anon. (1874). The Late Dr. Edwin Lankester and Medical Coroners. *MTG*, 2, 525.
9. Anon. (1875). Edwin Lankester. *Nature*, 11, 15.
10. Royal College of Physicians. *Annals* (mss.), 23, 55. Held at the College.
11. Cope, Z. (1966). The Private Medical Schools of London, 1746-1914. In Poynter, F. N. L. (ed.), *The Evolution of Medical Education in Britain*. London: Pitman.
12. Lankester, E. (1845). *Report of Lectures on the Natural History of Plants Yielding Food*. London: Churchill. Title page.
13. Loudon, I. S. L. (1981). The Origins and Growth of the Dispensary Movement in England. *Bull. Hist. Med.*, 55, 322.
14. Loudon, I. S. L. Personal communication.
15. Royal College of Physicians. *Annals* (mss.), 23, 253. Held at the College.
16. Davenport, G. (Librarian, Royal College of Physicians). Personal communication.
17. Lankester, E. (1841-1844). Letters to G. Long and E. Conoley. Held in the Archives of University College, London.
18. Weisart, Dr. (Ruprecht-Karls-Universität, Heidelberg). Personal communication.

Chapter 4. Fellow of the Linnean Society

General sources.   Howarth, O. J. R. (1922). *The British Association for the Advancement of Science. A Retrospect. 1831-1931.* London.
Annual Reports of the British Association for the Advancement of Science, 1837-1844.

1. *Report of the B.A.A.S., Liverpool* (1937). 6.
2. Morrell, J. and Thackray, A. (1981). *Gentlemen of Science. Early years of the British Association for the Advancement of Science*. Oxford: Clarendon Press.

3. E. Lankester's Certificate of Candidature for Fellowship of the Royal Society (1845). Held in the Society's Archives.

4. *Report of the B. A. A. S., Birmingham* (1839). **8**, 78.

5. Wilson, G. and Geikie, A. (1861). *A Memoir of Edward Forbes.* Edinburgh.

6. Allen, D. E. (1975). *The Naturalist in Britain. A Social History.* London: Allen Lane, 46.

7. Ibid., 137.

8. Lankester, E. Papers and letters in the Archives of the Linnean Society of London.

9. Lankester, E. (1838-1848). On a White Incrustation on Stones from the bed of the River Annan produced by *Synedra ulna. Proc. Linn. Soc.,* **1**, 81.

10. Peculiar Structure of Cells on the Surface of *Callitriche nema.* Ibid., (1848-1855). **2**, 94.

11. Morrell, J. Personal communication.

12. Lankester, E. (1844-1847). Letters to William Jardine. Held at the Royal Scottish Museum, Edinburgh.

13. Lankester, E. (1844). *First Annual Report of the Ray Society.* Bound with the author's translation of H. F. Link's *Report on the Progress of Physiological Botany during 1841.* Copy in Linnean Society Library.

14. Anon. (1846). *Memorials of John Ray. Athenaeum,* 704.

15. Raven, C. E. (1950). *John Ray, Naturalist,* Cambridge.

16. Marriage Certificate of Edwin Lankester and Phebe Pope.

17. Anon. (1909). Lankester, Edwin. *DNB,* **11**, 578.

18. Lindley, J. (1846). Lankesteria parviflora. *Bot. Register,* **32**, tab. 12.

Chapter 5. Thwarted Physician

General sources.   Owen, D. (1982). *The Government of Victorian London, 1855-1889.* Cambridge, Mass.: Harvard University Press.

Manuscript Minutes of the Vestry of St. James's, Westminster. Held in the Victoria Library, Westminster.

Lancet, BMJ and *MTG* for the period.

1. Royal College of Physicians. *Annals* (mss.), **24**, 112-114. Held at the College.

2. Crisp, E. (1874). The Late Dr. Lankester. *BMJ,* **2**, 666.

3. Lankester, E. (1849). Letters dated 2.8.49 and 4.8.49 in College Correspondence; also Council Report no. 51. Held in the Archives of University College, London.

4. Forster, J. (1966). *Life and Letters of Charles Dickens*, Dent. 2, 52.

5. Lankester, P. (1889-1890). Letters in Archives of Dickens House Museum.

6. *Punch* (1849). 25 August, 76.

7. *London Medical Gazette*, 1849-1851.

8. Loudon, I. S. L. Personal Communication.

9. Swarbrick, M. J. (Victoria Library, Westminster). Personal communication.

10. Minutes of the Vestry of St. James's, Westminster, 2 June, 1841.

11. Lankester, E. (1851). In *New College, London. Introductory Lectures*.

12. New College, London. Minutes of Council, No.1, 1850. Held in Dr. Williams's Library, London.

13. Lankester, E. (1847-8). The Natural History of Creation. *Lectures: Young Men's Christian Association*.

14. Passing references in *Medical Directory*, *Lancet*, etc.

15. Lankester, E. (1849). Application for physiciancy at University College Hospital. See Chap. 3, 1.

16. Lankester, E. (1850). School of Medicine and Anatomy. *Medical Times*, **20**, 352-358.

17. Anon. (1850). The studies of the Medical Man. *Athanaeum*, 1187.

18. Pelling, M. (1978). *Cholera, Fever and English Medicine, 1825-1865*. O.U.P., 154.

19. *Report of the B.A.A.S., Ipswich*, (1851). **9**.

20. Anon. (1929). Man who made Science Simple. *East Anglian Daily Times*, 19 August.

21. J. F. P. (1875). The Late Dr. Lankester. *Q.J.M.Sc.*, **15**, 59.

22. Sillett, R. E. W. (1956). *Edwin Lankester*, Thesis for the Degree of M.D. in the University of Birmingham.

23. Anon. (1874). Edwin Lankester, M.D., M.R.C.P., F.R.S. *Lancet*, **2**, 676.

24. Meynell, G. (1980). The Royal Botanic Society's Garden, Regent's Park. *Lond.J.*, **6**, 135.

25. Royal Botanic Society of London., *Reports, 1850-1855*, Held in St. Marylebone Public Library.

26. Michael, A. D. (1895). The President's Address. *J. Royal Micr. Soc.*, 16.

Chapter 6. Cholera.

1. Finer, S. E. (1952). *The Life and Times of Sir Edwin Chadwick*. London: Methuen, 346-7.
2. Bulloch, W. (1938). *The History of Bacteriology*. Oxford University Press.
3. Ainsworth, G. C. (1987). *Introduction to the History of Medical and Veterinary Mycology*. Cambridge University Press, 153.
4. Eyler, J. M. (1979). *Victorian Social Medicine: the Ideas and Methods of William Farr*. Johns Hopkins University, 97-108.
5. Pelling, M. (1978). *Cholera, Fever and English Medicine, 1825-1865*. O.U.P., 100-107.
6. Frazer, W. M. (1950). *A History of Public Health*. London: Baillière, Tyndall and Cox, 69.
7. Richardson, B. W. (1949). A Biographical Memoir. In *Snow on Cholera, Being a Reprint of Two Papers of John Snow*.
8. Snow, John (1855). On the Mode of Communication of Cholera. In *Snow on Cholera*, as above.
9. Goodall, E. W. (1936). *William Budd, M.D. Edin., F.R.S.* Bristol: Arrowsmith.
10. Pelling, M. (1978). As (5) above, 146-211.
11. Lankester, E. (1849). The Bodies Found in Cholera Evacuations. *Lancet*, 2, 460.
12. Lankester, E. (1849). On the Progress of Organic Chemistry. In *Companion to the Alamanac, or Yearbook of General Information*. London.
13. Lankester, E. (1849). In: Report of the Meeting of Westminster Medical Society, *Lancet*, 2, 404.
14. Berkeley, M. J. (1849). On the larger cells observed in cholera evacuations by J. G. Swayne Esq. M.D., Dr. Budd and others. *Lond. Med. Gaz.*, 9, 1035-7.
15. Member of the Bristol Microscopical Society (1849). The Bristol Microscopical Society *versus* the President of the Microscopical Society of London. *Lancet*, 2, 460.
16. Finer, S. E. (1952). As (1) above, 392.
17. Clayton, E. G. (1908). *Arthur Hill Hassell, Physician and Sanitary Reformer*. London: Baillière, Tyndall and Cox.
18. Lankester, E. (1852). In Lankester, E. and Redfern, P. *Reports made to the Directors of the London (Watford) Spring Water Company*.
19. Lankester, E. and Redfern, P. (1852). The Microscope as a test of the Purity of Drinking Water. *Lancet*, 2, 353.
20. Finer, S. E. (1952). As (1) above, 458.
21. Minutes of the Vestry of St. James's, Westminster, (1854-1855). **6.**

22. Chave, S. P. W. (1958). Henry Whitehead and Cholera in Broad Street. *Med. Hist.*, **2**, 92.
23. Lankester, E. (1856). On the Presence of Microscopic Fungi in Water Deleterious to Health. *Q.J.M.Sc.*, **4**, 270.
24. Vestry of St. James's, Westminster (1855). *Report on the Cholera Outbreak during the Autumn of 1854*. London; Churchill.
25. Anon. (1855). The Report of the Cholera Outbreak at St. James's, Westminster. *J. Publ. Hlth. Sanitary Rev*, **1**, 396.
26. Brockington, C. F. (1965). *Public Health in the Nineteenth Century*. Livingstone, 197-204.

Chapter 7. Medical Politician

General sources. Waddington, I. (1984). *The Medical Profession in the Industrial Revolution*. Dublin: Gill and MacMillan.
Little, E.M. (1932). *History of the British Medical Association, 1832-1932*. London: B.M.A..
AMJ, 1853-6.   *Lancet*, 1853-8.
BMJ, 1857-8.   *MTG*, 1853-8.

1. McMenemey, W. H. (1966). Education and the Medical Reform Movement. In: Poynter, F.N.L., *Evolution of Medical Education in Britain*, London: Pitman Medical, 147.
2. Anon. (1853). London Medical Reform Committee. *MTG*, 1, 588.
3. Lankester, E. (1854). In: Association Intelligence. *AMJ*, 869.
4. Anon. (1865). Meeting of the Provincial Medical and Surgical Association at York. *MTG*, 2, 193.
5. A Provincial (1855). The Provincial Medical and Surgical Association and its Metropolitan Branch. *Lancet*, 2, 477.
6. Anon. (1855). The Birmingham Meeting of the Provincial Medical and Surgical Association. *MTG*, 522.
7. Lankester, E. (1857). In: Association Intelligence. *BMJ*, 2, 673.
8. Anon. (1855). Provincial Medical and Surgical Association. Report of the Medical Reform Committee. *AMJ*, 782.
9. Lankester, E. (1855). As above, 783.
10. Lankester, E. (1856). Provincial Medical and Surgical Association. Report of the Medical Reform Committee. *AMJ*, 523.
11. Budd, W. (1857). In: Meeting of the British Medical Association at Nottingham. *BMJ*, 672.
12. Lankester, E. (1858). In: Report of Meeting of the Metropolitan Counties Branch. *BMJ*, 911.

Chapter 8. Interlude

1. Anon. (1874). Edwin Lankester, M.D., M.R.C.P., F.R.S. *Lancet*, **2**, 676.
2. Anon. (1887). Clark, Sir James. *DNB*, **10**, 401.
3. Hobhouse, H. (1983). *Prince Albert: His Life and Work*. London: Hamish Hamilton, 139.
4. Anon. (1842). Editorial. *Lancet*, **42** (2), 455.
5. Lankester, E. (1854). Letter to William Hooker. No. 151, William Hooker, English Letters. Kew Archives.
6. Now in the Royal Archives, Windsor Castle.
7. Sillett, R. E. W. (1956). *Edwin Lankester*. Thesis for the Degree of M.D. in the University of Birmingham
8. de Bellaigue, Lady S. (Deputy Registrar, Royal Archives). Personal communication.
9. Lankester, E. (1856). On the presence of microscopic fungi in water deleterious to health. *Q.J.M.Sc.*, **4**, 270 and Pl. 14.
10. English, M. P. (1986). Robert Hardwicke (1822-1875), publisher of biological and medical books. *Arch. Nat. Hist.*, **13**, 25.
11. Anon. (1856). *Report of the Meeting of the Worcestershire Natural History Society, 1856*. Pamphlet bound with *Worcestershire Natural History Society, 1853-1836*.
12. Ibid., 1857.
13. Lankester, P. (1889-1890). Letters in Archives of Dickens House Museum.

Chapter 9. Medical Officer of Health

General sources. Wohl, A. (1983). *Endangered Lives. Public Health in Victorian Britain*. London: Dent.
Minutes of the Vestry of St. James's, Westminster, 1856-1859.
Reports of the MOH to the Vestry of St. James's Westminster, 1856- 1872-3.

1. Lankester, E. (1860). Measures for the improvement of the public health - water supply and drainage. *TNAPSSc.*, 666.
2. Anon. (1855). Leading Article. *Lancet*, **2**, 284.
3. Lankester, E., Annual Report, 1856.
4. Lankester, E., Annual Report, 1857.
5. Lankester, E. (1868). On overcrowding. *BMJ*, **2**, 208.
6. Anon. (1865). Monthly Chronicle. *J.Soc. Sci.*, **1**, 547

7. Lankester, E. Annual Report, 1858.
8. Lankester, E. (1858). The drinking water of the metropolis. *BMJ*, 134.
9. Anon. (1861). Professional testimonial mongers. *BMJ*, 2, 415.
10. Lankester, E. (1861). Letter. *BMJ*, 2, 451.
11. Lankester, E. Annual Report, 1863.
12. Lankester, E. (1870). The Smallpox epidemic. *Nature*, 3, 341.
13. Lankester, E. (1870). The present epidemic of scarlet fever. *Nature*, 3, 41.
14. Lankester, E. (1870). Letter. *Nature*, 3, 125.

Chapter 10. Professional Groups

General source. *TNAPSSc.*, 1857-1870.

1. Dudfield, R. (1906). History of the Society of Medical Officers of Health. *Public Health*, 18, 1-133.
2. Lankester, E. (1862). The causation of typhoid fever. *BMJ*, 1, 273.
3. Budd, W. (1855). On the fever at the clergy orphan asylum. *Lancet*, 2, 617.
4. Budd, W. (1856). On intestinal fever; its mode of propogation. *Lancet*, 2, 694.
5. Millman, M. (1974). The influence of the Social Science Association on hospital planning in Victorian England. *Med. Hist.*, 18, 122.
6. Lankester, E. (1865). In: Report of the Ninth Annual Meeting of the Association, *J. Soc. Sci.*, 1, 33.
7. Anon. (1867). Notes for a History of Sanitary Legislation. *MTG*, 1, 379.

Chapter 11. South Kensington

General sources.   Manuscript Minutes of the Department of Science and Art. ED 28, 1858-1863. Public Record Office, Kew.
House of Commons Parliamentary Papers. Reports of the Science and Art Department. 1859-1864.

1. English, M. P. (1977). William Tilbury Fox and dermatological mycology. *Br. J. Derm.*, 97, 573.
2. Berman, M. (1978). *Social Change and Scientific Organisation: the Royal Institution, 1799-1844.* London: Heinemann Educational.

3. Lankester, E. (1858). Reports of Societies. Royal Institution. *MTG*, **1**, 512, 565.

4. Lankester, E. (1858). Reports of Societies. Royal Institution. *MTG*, **2**, 20.

5. Anon. (1858). Report of Meeting of the British Association for the Advancement of Science. Ozonometer. *BMJ*, 878.

6. Anon. (1859). Metropolitan Association of Medical Officers of Health. *Lancet*, **1**, 347.

7. *International Exhibition of 1862. Official Illustrated Catalogue.*

8. Argles, M. (1964). *South Kensington to Robbins.* London: Longmans Green, 18-20.

9. Hobhouse, H. (1983). *Prince Albert, His Life and Work.* London: Hamish Hamilton. 109-114.

10. Follett, D. (1978). *The Rise of the Science Museum under Henry Lyons.* 1.

11. Butterworth, H. (1968). *The Science and Arts Department, 1853-1890.* Thesis for the Degree of Ph.D., Sheffield University.

12. Anon. (1856). Medical News. *MTG*, **1**, 586.

13. Anon. (1861). Reviews and Notices of Books. *Lancet*, **2**, 603.

14. Anon. (1862). *Athenaeum*, June 28, 850.

15. Letters from various authors (1861). *BMJ*, 360, 389, 451, 509, 514.

16. Lankester, E. (1873). Cookery at South Kensington. *Nature*, **8**, 178.

17. Lankester, E. (1859). The President's Address for the year 1859. *Trans. Micr. Soc. Lond.*, New ser. **7**, 64.

18. Lankester, E. (1860). The President's Address for the year 1860. *Trans. Micr. Soc. Lond.*, New ser. **8**, 83.

19. Lankester, E. (1859). *Sanitary Defects and Medical Shortcomings.* London.

20. English, M. P. (1987). *Mordecai Cubitt Cooke: Victorian Naturalist, Mycologist, Teacher and Eccentric.* Bristol: Biopress. p. 61.

21. Cooke, M. C. (1863, 1864). "Proceedings of the Society of Amateur Botanists". Manuscript in the Botany Library, Natural History Museum.

22. Cooke, M. C. (1898-1900). Early memories of the Q.M.C. *J. Quekett Micr. Club*, Ser. 2, **7**, 229.

23. Anon. (1865). *J. Quekett Micr. Club*, **1**, pages following p. 254.

Chapter 12. Coroner for Central Middlesex

General sources.   Knapman, P. and Powers, M.J. (1985). *The Law and Practice on Coroners*. Chichester: Barry Rose.
BMJ, 1862-1873.
Lancet, 1862-1873.
MTG, 1862-1873.
Minutes of the Committee Meetings of the Coroners' Society of England and Wales, 1862-1872.
Annual Reports of the Coroners' Society of England and Wales, 1862-1872.

1.   Anon. (1868). Election of Coroners. *BMJ*, 2, 254.
2.   Anon. (1863). Medical claims to the coronership. *Lancet*, 2, 76.
3.   Anon. (1862). The Week. *BMJ*, 2, 42.
4.   Advertisement. (1862). Dr. Lankester's election fund. *BMJ*, 2, 23.
5.   Lankester, E. (1866). Letter to the Editor. *Lancet*, 1, 696.
6.   Anon. (1862). Health of St. James's. *Lancet*, 2, 292.
7.   Anon. (1862). The salary of the Coroner for the Central Division of Middlesex. *Lancet*, 2, 299.
8.   Anon. (1864). Coroner Lankester's First Annual Report. *MTG*, 1, 563.
9.   Anon. (1865). The Coroner's Court and Dr. Lankester's Second Annual Report. *MTG*, 1, 443.
10. Anon. (1866). Third Annual Report of the Coroner for Central Middlesex. *BMJ*, 1, 448.
11. Anon. (1865). The Coroner's Court and Dr. Lankester's Second Annual Report. *MTG*, 1, 443.
12. Anon. (1866). Third Report of the Coroner for Central Middlesex. *MTG*, 1, 368.
13. Anon. (1864). Dr. Lankester on *post mortem* examinations. *BMJ*, 2, 345.
14. Anon. (1867). The Fourth Report of the Coroner for Central Middlesex. *Lancet*, 1, 255.
15. Anon. (1867). The Health Section of the Social Science Congress at Belfast. *MTG*, 2, 410.
16. Anon. (1872). The duty of the Coroner. *MTG*, 1, 165.
17. Anon. (1865). Medical Certificate of Death. *J. Soc. Sci.*, 1, 546.
18. Lankester, E. (1867). The Registration systems. Discussion. *TNAPSSc.*, 548.
19. Lankester, E. (1869). *Sixth Annual Report of the Coroner for Central Middlesex*. London: Hardwicke.
20. Lankester, E. (1864). In: Health Department. Summary of Proceedings. *TNAPSSc.*, 581.

21. Lankester, E. (1870). The representation of Science at the School Board. *Nature*, **2**, 509.
22. Anon. (1859). Leading Article. *Lancet*, **1**, 244.
23. Anon. (1873). A medical Coroner's vindication. *MTG*, **1**, 470.
24. Anon. (1873). The Middlesex Magistrates and Dr. Lankester. *Lancet*, **2**, 644.
25. Anon. (1869). The Coronership for West Middlesex. *MTG*, **1**, 468.
26. Anon. (1871). Seventh Annual Report of the Coroner for the Central Division of Middlesex. *MTG*, **1**, 130.

Chapter 13. Overwork and Anxiety.

1. Lankester, E. Papers and letters in the Archives of the Linnean Society of London.
2. Correspondence of William Carruthers, in the Botany Library, Natural History Museum.
3. New College, London, Minutes of Council, No. 1: also Lankester correspondence. Held in Dr. Williams's Library, London.
4. English, M.P. (1987). *Mordecai Cubitt Cooke: Victorian Naturalist, Mycologist, Teacher and Eccentric*. Bristol: Biopress, p. 88.
5. Anon. (1874). Obituary. Edwin Lankester, M.D., F.R.C.P., F.R.S.. *Lancet*, **2**, 676.
6. Anon. (1874). Obituary. Edwin Lankester, M.D., M.R.C.P., F.R.S.. *BMJ*, **2**, 603.
7. J. F. P. (1875). The late Dr. Lankester. *Q.J.M.Sc.*, **15**, 59.

Postscript

1. Anon. (1874). Editorial. *Lancet*, **2**, 771.
2. Anon. (1900). Obituary. Phebe Lankester. *Times*, April 14.
3. National Health Society. Sixth Annual Report. (1879).
4. Information from a Lankester family tree held at Ipswich Museum.
5. Anon. (1934). Lankester, Edward Forbes, Q.C. *Who was Who*, 1929-1940.
6. Anon. (1934). Alfred Owen Lankester. *Lancet*, **1**, 56.

Index